Jackie

522-4212

Simple Truths

The Best of The Cockle Bur

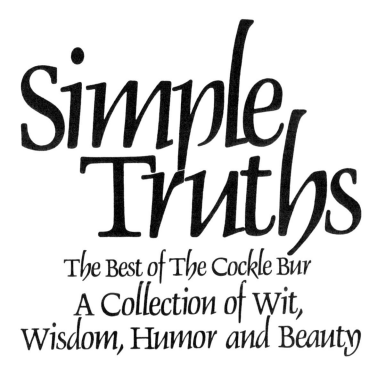

Simple Truths

The Best of The Cockle Bur
A Collection of Wit, Wisdom, Humor and Beauty

Compiled and edited by Harry B. Otis

Illustrated by Larri Munderloh

Andrews and McMeel
A Universal Press Syndicate Company

Kansas City • New York

Library of Congress Cataloging-in-Publication Data

Otis, Harry B.
  Simple truths : the best of the cockle bur : a collection of wit, wisdom, humor, and beauty / compiled and edited by Harry B. Otis.
    p.   cm.
  Previous collection published in 1987 under title: The best of the cockle bur.
  Includes index.
  ISBN 0–8362–7983–2 $8.95
  1. Quotations. 2. Wit and humor. I. Otis, Harry B. Best of the cockle bur. II. Title.
PN6084.H808   1990
082—dc20
                                                          90–43075
                                                          CIP

FOREWORD

Poor Richard said:
> *"If you would not be forgotten as soon as you are dead and rotten, either write things worth reading or do things worth the writing."*

In 1930 Albert and Eda Cockle did "something worth the writing" in promoting their ten-year-old law brief printing company. They created *The Cockle Bur,* an eight-page brochure containing quotes, jokes, and items of interest. The work also included poems to entertain the reader and to highlight the change of season. Every month the Cockles mailed this booklet to lawyer customers and friends, who, delighted, soon joined in the quest for material for the next issue.

Fifty-seven years later, Cockle descendants continue to print this monthly pamphlet. George Cockle carried on the promotion after his parents had departed the scene. Today it is George's daughter, Cindy Vercruysse, who pursues the tedious hunt for acceptable tidbits.

Fortunately, copies of all these *Cockle Burs* were saved, some by a friend and a former customer. From a gold mine of nearly half a century this retired attorney has extracted the contents of the present work. He presents these nuggets in the traditional *Cockle Bur* format, dividing the material, however, into seasons rather than months. As a novel touch, Omaha artist Larri Munderloh has sprinkled the book's contents with her pen and ink sketches.

Simple Truths is meant to be a keeper. Please place it on your permanent library shelf to be pulled down from time to time for a chuckle, a reflection, or, perhaps, a speech.

Harry B. Otis
Omaha, Nebraska

DEDICATED TO

THE MEMORY OF

ALBERT AND EDA COCKLE

CONTENTS

SPRING

Spring . .

This is the time between the sleep and the waking, when the wind softens and winter's sullen moods, follies and cold humors pass. It is in the air, the change that will not be denied, the earth's compliant yielding to spring.

The horse gallops in the sodden meadow, the warm coddling sun stirs the wild ginger, the dog runs yelping along the river's edge. The sense of yesterday slowly expires as new life comes out of old decay.

♦ ♦ ♦

A good, contented, well-breakfasted juryman, is a capital thing to get hold of. Discontented or hungry jurymen, my dear sir, always find for the plaintiff.   —Charles Dickens

♦ ♦ ♦

For there was never yet philosopher
That could endure the toothache patiently.
                              —William Shakespeare

♦ ♦ ♦

A Texan was trying to impress upon a Bostonian the valor of the heroes of the Alamo.

"I'll bet you never had anybody so brave around Boston," said the Texan.

"Did you ever hear of Paul Revere?" asked the Bostonian.

"Paul Revere?" said the Texan. "Isn't that the guy who ran for help?"

♦ ♦ ♦

Hospitality is commended to be exercised, even toward an enemy, when he cometh to thine house. The tree does not withdraw its shadow, even for the woodcutter.   —Chinese Proverb

No one would ever have crossed the ocean if he could have gotten off the ship in the storm.

—Sign in Charles F. Kettering's office

♦ ♦ ♦

A highbrow is a person educated beyond his intelligence.

—Brander Matthews

♦ ♦ ♦

A critic is a legless man who teaches running.

—Channing Pollock

♦ ♦ ♦

"Positive"—mistaken at the top of one's voice.

—Ambrose Bierce

♦ ♦ ♦

Oats—A grain which in England is generally given to horses, but in Scotland supports the people. —Samuel Johnson

♦ ♦ ♦

What is a cynic? A man who knows the price of everything, and the value of nothing. —Oscar Wilde

♦ ♦ ♦

It is hard to believe a man is telling the truth when you know that you would lie if you were in his place. —H.L. Mencken

♦ ♦ ♦

The biggest bells in England have personal names. Here are the names of the seven largest, with their locations: "Big Ben," Westminster Palace; "Great Paul," St. Paul's Cathedral; "Great Peter," Yorkminster; "Little John," Nottingham; "Tom," Christ Church, Oxford; "Tom," Lincoln Cathedral; and "Great George," Bristol University.

♦ ♦ ♦

Have a care where there is more sail than ballast.

—William Penn

4

The excesses of contemporary business writing bring to mind Cornelius Vanderbilt, who wrote my favorite business letter:

"Gentlemen: You have undertaken to cheat me. I won't sue you, for the law is too slow. I'll ruin you.　　　　Yours truly,
Cornelius Vanderbilt"

◆ ◆ ◆

Before Coolidge left the White House, his Vermont neighbors decided to recognize his devotion to the old farm by giving him a hand-made rake.

They made the presentation an elaborate ceremonial. The orator who presented the rake dwelt on the qualities of the hickory wood from which he said it was made.

"Hickory," he said, "like the President, is sturdy, strong, resilient, unbroken." And so on and on and on. Then he handed the rake to Mr. Coolidge, and the audience settled back for the speech of acknowledgment.

The President turned the implement over, scrutinized it carefully, and then made his address in a single word.

"Ash," he said.

◆ ◆ ◆

It's just as unpleasant to get more than you bargain for as to get less.　　　　—George Bernard Shaw

◆ ◆ ◆

Memory is what a motorist uses to almost find the right way.

◆ ◆ ◆

Make three correct guesses consecutively and you will establish a reputation as an expert.　　　　—Laurence Peter

◆ ◆ ◆

To add a library to a house is to give that house a soul. —Cicero

Charles A. Beard, dean of American historians, died at the age of 73. When asked at one time if he could summarize the lessons of history in a short book, Mr. Beard said he could do it in four sentences:

1. Whom the gods would destroy, they first make mad with power.
2. The mills of God grind slowly, but they grind exceedingly small.
3. The bee fertilizes the flower it robs.
4. When it is dark enough, you can see the stars.

♦ ♦ ♦

One of the recent Broadhurst stories concerned the Frenchman walking the streets of London, studying English, trying to pronounce though, rough, cough, hiccough, plow, and through. He happened to look up and saw an electric sign: "Cavalcade, Pronounced Success!" So he gave it up and went back to Marseilles.

♦ ♦ ♦

Democracy in America, 1835 . . .
There are at the present time two great nations in the world . . . the Russians and the Americans. . . . The American relies upon personal interest to accomplish his ends and gives free scope to the unguided exertions and common sense of the people. The Russian centers all the authority of society in a single arm. The principal instrument of the former is freedom; of the latter servitude. Their starting point is different, and their courses are not the same; yet each of them seems marked out by the will of Heaven to sway the destinies of half the globe.　　　　　—Alexis de Tocqueville

♦ ♦ ♦

If you'd lose a troublesome visitor lend him money.
　　　　　　　　　　　　　　　　—Benjamin Franklin

6

When you see a married couple coming down the street, the one who is two or three steps ahead is the one that's mad.

—Helen Rowland

♦ ♦ ♦

Neither a borrower, nor a lender be;
For loan oft loses both itself and friend,
And borrowing dulls the edge of husbandry.
This above all: to thine own self be true,
And it must follow, as the night the day,
Thou canst not then be false to any man.   —William Shakespeare

♦ ♦ ♦

Twelve things to remember: The value of time, the success of perseverance, the pleasure of working, the dignity of simplicity, the worth of character, the power of kindness, the influence of example, the obligation of duty, the wisdom of economy, the virtue of patience, the improvement of talent, and the joy of originating.   —Marshall Field

♦ ♦ ♦

Economists report that a college education adds many thousands of dollars to a man's lifetime income—which he then spends sending his son to college.   —Bill Vaughan

♦ ♦ ♦

The Lord is my Shepherd; I shall not want.

He maketh me to lie down in green pastures; he leadeth me beside the still waters.

He restoreth my soul: he leadeth me in the paths of righteousness for his name's sake.

Yea, though I walk through the valley of the shadow of death, I will fear no evil: for thou art with me; thy rod and thy staff they comfort me.

Thou preparest a table before me in the presence of mine enemies; thou anointest my head with oil; my cup runneth over.

Surely goodness and mercy shall follow me all the days of my life; and I will dwell in the house of the Lord for ever.   —Psalm 23

Some praise at morning what they blame at night,
But always think the last opinion right.   —Alexander Pope

♦ ♦ ♦

It rarely enlarges
My head, but flattery
Surely recharges
My ego's battery!   —Georgie Starbuck Galbraith

♦ ♦ ♦

"You're entitled to your opinion,"
    He'll tell you on the spot,
But from the way he says it,
    You sorta feel you're not.

                                —Stephen Schlitzer

♦ ♦ ♦

If I were to pray for a taste which would stand me in stead under
every variety of circumstances, and be a source of happiness and
cheerfulness to me through life, and a shield against its ills,
however things might go amiss, and the world frown upon me, it
would be a taste for reading.   —Sir John Herschel

♦ ♦ ♦

There is a tide in the affairs of men
Which taken at the flood leads on to fortune;
Omitted, all the voyage of their life
Is bound in shallows and in miseries.
On such a full sea are we now afloat,
And we must take the current when it serves,
Or lose our ventures.   —William Shakespeare

Avoid popularity; it has many snares and no real benefits.
—William Penn

♦ ♦ ♦

A man's worst difficulties begin when he is able to do as he likes.
—T.H. Huxley

♦ ♦ ♦

Material abundance without character is the surest way to destruction.
—Thomas Jefferson

♦ ♦ ♦

It costs more now to amuse a child than it used to cost to educate his father.

♦ ♦ ♦

The most quoted stanzas in Longfellow's "A Psalm of Life" are these:

> Lives of great men all remind us
> We can make our lives sublime.
> And, departing, leave behind us
> Footprints on the sands of time.
>
> Let us, then, be up and doing,
> With a heart for any fate;
> Still achieving, still pursuing,
> Learn to labor and to wait.

What interests us at the moment is the last line. If there is one bit of advice the young people of this nation seem to need above all else, it is to be patient. The wives need to "learn to labor and to wait" as much as their husbands. Everybody is in too big a hurry to get somewhere. Sometimes success comes suddenly, but usually after long years of tedious effort.

I wandered lonely as a Cloud
That floats on high o'er Vales and Hills,
When all at once I saw a crowd
A host of dancing Daffodils;
Along the Lake, beneath the trees,
Ten thousand dancing in the breeze.

The waves beside them danced, but they
Outdid the sparkling waves in glee:—
A Poet could not but be gay
In such a laughing company:
I gazed—and gazed—but little thought
What wealth the shew to me had brought:

For oft when on my couch I lie
In vacant or in pensive mood.
They flash upon that inward eye
Which is the bliss of solitude,
And then my heart with pleasure fills,
And dances with the Daffodils.   —William Wordsworth

♦ ♦ ♦

Triumph is just umph added to try.

♦ ♦ ♦

Vows begin when hope dies.   —Leonardo da Vinci

♦ ♦ ♦

May you live all the days of your life.   —Jonathan Swift

♦ ♦ ♦

A quiet, serious, sensible guest will just about ruin a modern party.

The French are true romantics. They feel the only difference between a man of forty and one of seventy is thirty years of experience. —Maurice Chevalier

♦ ♦ ♦

When you rise in the morning, form a resolution to make the day a happy one to a fellow-creature. —Sydney Smith

♦ ♦ ♦

A man's treatment of money is the most decisive test of his character—how he makes it and how he spends it.
—James Moffatt

♦ ♦ ♦

The operator was about to close the doors of the crowded elevator when a tipsy gentleman pushed his way in. As the car started up he tried to turn around to face the door, but was wedged in so tightly that he couldn't move. The other passengers stared into his rather bleary eyes with growing embarrassment. Finally, when the strain became quite painful, the tipsy one cleared his throat and remarked, "I expect you are wondering why I called this meeting."

♦ ♦ ♦

Only people who do things get criticized.

♦ ♦ ♦

The fishing party was hopelessly lost in deep woods, with supplies running low. "I thought you claimed to be the best guide in Wisconsin," said one man. "I am," shrugged the guide, "but now I think we're somewhere in Manitoba."

11

No man is an island, entire of itself; every man is a piece of the continent, a part of the main; if a clod be washed away by the sea, Europe is the less, as well as if a promontory were, as well as if a manor of thy friends or of thine own were; any man's death diminishes me, because I am involved in mankind; and therefore never send to know for whom the bell tolls; it tolls for thee.

—John Donne

♦ ♦ ♦

If we imagine that the whole of the Earth's history were compressed into a single year, then on this scale, the first 8 months would be completely without life. The following 2 months would be devoted to the most primitive of creatures, ranging from viruses and single-celled bacteria to jelly-fish, while the mammals would not appear until the second week in December. Man as we know him would have strutted onto the stage at about 1:45 p.m. on December 31st, and the age of written history would have occupied little more than the last 60 seconds on the clock.

—Richard Carrington

♦ ♦ ♦

That man is a success who has lived well, laughed often and loved much; who has gained the respect of intelligent men and the love of children; who has filled his niche and accomplished his task; who leaves the world better than he found it, whether by an improved poppy, a perfect poem, or a rescued soul; who never lacked appreciation of earth's beauty or failed to express it; who looked for the best in others and gave the best he had.

—Robert Louis Stevenson

♦ ♦ ♦

Columnist Abigail Van Buren told a Washington audience her favorite recent letter said: "Dear Abby: I joined the Navy to see the world. I've seen it. Now, how do I get out?"

12

Every person has the power to make others happy; one does it simply by entering a room—others, by leaving the room.

I have a friend who leaves a trail of enthusiasm. Hours after a telephone call from him I still feel great.

Another friend leaves a trail of optimism. After only a brief conversation with him I feel better. He always makes my day.

One friend enriches my day by always leaving a trail of kindness. Cheerful smiles are his trademark.

Some individuals leave trails of gloom; others, trails of joy. Some leave trails of hate and bitterness; others, trails of love and harmony.

Some leave trails of cynicism and pessimism; others, trails of faith and optimism. Some leave trails of criticism and resignation; others, trails of gratitude and hope.

What kinds of trails do you leave?   —William Arthur Ward

♦ ♦ ♦

Fishing philosophy times three: (1) The two best times to fish are when it's rainin' and when it ain't. (2) There ain't no property you can't fish if you know how to sit a spell with the man that owns it. (3) Any time a man ain't fishin', he's fritterin' away his time.

♦ ♦ ♦

My wife and I tried two or three times in the last forty years to have breakfast together, but it was so disagreeable we had to stop.
        —Winston Churchill

♦ ♦ ♦

A Protestant boy wanted to marry a Catholic girl whose parents felt it would be advisable for the lad to adopt the family religion. He began to read the proper literature and attend classes taught by the parish priest.

All went well until one day the mother came home to find her daughter sobbing her heart out.

"It's . . . it's Paul," the girl wailed. "There isn't going to be any wedding." "What ever is the matter, darling? Doesn't he love you anymore?"

"It isn't that," the daughter explained. "We . . . we oversold him! He's going to become a priest."

13

April cold with dropping rain
Willows and lilacs bring again,
The whistle of returning birds,
And trumpet-lowing of the herds;
The scarlet maple-keys betray
What potent blood hath modest May;
What fiery force the earth renews,
The wealth of forms, the flush of hues;
What Joy in rosy waves outpoured,
Flows, from the heart of Love, the Lord.

—Ralph Waldo Emerson

♦ ♦ ♦

It ain't so much the things that people don't know that makes trouble in this world, as it is the things that people know that ain't so. —Mark Twain

♦ ♦ ♦

It is not enough merely to exist. It's not enough to say, "I'm earning enough to live and to support my family. I do my work well. I'm a good father. I'm a good husband. I'm a good church-goer." That's all very well. But you must do something more. Seek always to do some good, somewhere. Every man has to seek in his own way to make his own self more noble and to realize his own true worth. You must give some time to your fellowman. Even if it's a little thing, do something for those who have a need of a man's help, something for which you get no pay but the privilege of doing it. For remember, you don't live in a world all your own. Your brothers are here, too. —Albert Schweitzer

♦ ♦ ♦

Have patience and the mulberry leaf will become satin.

—Spanish Proverb

♦ ♦ ♦

Repose is a good thing, but boredom is its brother. —Voltaire

14

If it were desired to crush a man completely, to punish him so severely that even the most hardened murderer would quail, it would only be needed to make his work absolutely pointless and absurd. —Fyodor Dostoyevski

♦ ♦ ♦

When Mrs. Stewart Edward White—who is half Spanish, half Scots, visited Scotland, a fine old gentleman of that land said to her: "Weel, weel, my dear, so ye hae Scottish bluid in ye! That gives ye a Scottish conscience. It won't keep ye from sinning; it just keeps ye from enjoyin' it!"

♦ ♦ ♦

He who smacks the head of every nail,
    Who misses not a trick,
Who always hits the bull's eye without fail—
    Makes me sick. —Addison H. Hallock

♦ ♦ ♦

Do not be fooled into believing that because a man is rich he is necessarily smart. There is ample proof to the contrary.
—Julius Rosenwald

♦ ♦ ♦

Our greatest glory is not in never falling but in rising every time we fall. —Confucius

♦ ♦ ♦

Always behave like a duck—keep calm and unruffled on the surface but paddle like the devil underneath.
—Lord Brabazon

Coroner: "And what were your husband's last words?"

Widow: "He said: 'I don't see how they can make any profit on this stuff at a dollar a quart.'"

♦ ♦ ♦

"I got this bottle of brandy for my mother-in-law."
"Say, what a marvelous exchange!"

♦ ♦ ♦

If you would like to leave footprints in the sands of time, you had better wear work shoes.　　　　—Herbert V. Prochnow

♦ ♦ ♦

Cub Reporter: "I'd like some advice, sir, on how to run a newspaper." Editor: "You've come to the wrong person, son. Ask one of my subscribers."

♦ ♦ ♦

"Love keeps the cold out better than a cloak."
　　　　　　　　　—Henry Wadsworth Longfellow

♦ ♦ ♦

Policeman: And just how did the accident happen?
Meek Motorist: My wife fell asleep in the back seat.

♦ ♦ ♦

"The only victory over love is flight."　　　　—Napoleon I

♦ ♦ ♦

Always be tolerant with those who disagree with you. After all, they have a perfect right to their ridiculous opinions.

16

The best thing about the future is that it comes only one day at a time.

♦ ♦ ♦

Sometimes one pays most fo the things one gets for nothing.
—Albert Einstein

♦ ♦ ♦

Failure is a far better teacher than success, but she hardly ever finds any apples on her desk.

♦ ♦ ♦

He is the happiest, be he king or peasant, who finds peace in his home.
—Johann Wolfgang von Goethe

♦ ♦ ♦

To me—old age is 15 years older than I am.
—Bernard M. Baruch

♦ ♦ ♦

If thine enemy wrong thee, buy each of his children a drum. —Chinese Proverb

♦ ♦ ♦

If you can't keep up with a conversation, keep out of it.

♦ ♦ ♦

The truly great are alwus the eazyest tew approach.
—Josh Billings

♦ ♦ ♦

Business is a combination of war and sport. —André Maurois

Before you complain about America, remember it's the only place where people don't want to move to another country.

—Adrian Anderson

♦ ♦ ♦

A man can succeed at almost anything for which he has unlimited enthusiasm.

—Charles Schwab

♦ ♦ ♦

Maxfield Parrish (1870–1966) specialized in painting beautiful nudes and was thus accustomed to having lovely young models in his studio. One morning, when a model arrived, Parrish suggested that they have a cup of coffee before getting down to work—a habit he had recently acquired to postpone confronting the blank canvas. They had hardly started to drink the coffee when the studio buzzer rang. Panic seized the artist. "Young lady," he cried, "for God's sake, take your clothes off—my wife's coming up to check on me."

♦ ♦ ♦

I think there is one smashing rule: Never face the facts.

—Ruth Gordon

♦ ♦ ♦

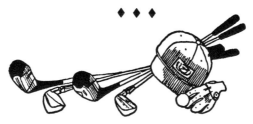

One of the quickest ways to meet new people is to pick up the wrong ball on the golf course.

♦ ♦ ♦

A perfectionist is a man who takes infinite pains and gives them to others.

—Alan Benner

♦ ♦ ♦

Virus is a Latin word used by doctors to mean "your guess is as good as mine."

—Bob Hope

18

L'ENVOI to "The Seven Seas"

When Earth's last picture is painted
  and the tubes are twisted and dried,
When the oldest colours have faded
  and the youngest critic has died,
We shall rest, and, faith, we shall need it—
  lie down for an aeon or two,
Till the Master of All Good Workmen
  shall put us to work anew.

And those that were good shall be happy:
  they shall sit in a golden chair;
They shall splash at a ten-league canvas
  with brushes of comets' hair.
They shall find real saints to draw from–
  Magdalene, Peter, and Paul;
They shall work for an age at a sitting
  and never be tired at all!

And only The Master shall praise us,
  and only The Master shall blame;
And no one shall work for money,
  and no one shall work for fame,
But each for the joy of the working,
  and each, in his separate star,
Shall draw the Thing as he sees It
  For the God of Things as They are!   —Rudyard Kipling

◆ ◆ ◆

The greatest and noblest pleasure which men can have in this world is to discover new truths; and the next is to shake off old prejudices.   —Frederick the Great

◆ ◆ ◆

Starting out to make money is the greatest mistake in life. Do what you feel you have a flair for doing, and if you are good enough at it the money will come.   —Lord Rootes

◆ ◆ ◆

There are three faithful friends—an old wife, an old dog, and ready money.   —Benjamin Franklin

I Shall Be Loved As Quiet Things . . .

I shall be loved as quiet things
Are loved—white pigeons in the sun,
Cured yellow leaves that whisper down
One after one;

The silver reticence of smoke
That tells no secret of its birth
Among the fiery agonies
That turn the earth,

Cloud-islands; reaching arms of trees;
The frayed and eager little moon
That stays unheeded through a high
Blue afternoon.

The thunder of my heart must go
Under the muffling of the dust—
As my grey dress has guarded it
The grasses must;

For it has hammered loud enough,
Clamored enough, when all is said:
Only its quiet part shall live
When I am dead.

—Karle Wilson Baker

♦ ♦ ♦

By appreciation we make excellence in others our own
property.   —Voltaire

♦ ♦ ♦

Because I do not understand how television works is no reason
why I cannot use it. The same may be said for the power of prayer.
I have seen so many answers to prayer that I do not doubt that
somehow one person's prayers can change the life or physical
condition of another person, even if the other person has no faith.
—Charles L. Allen

20

A poor blind woman in Paris put twenty-seven francs into a plate at a missionary meeting. "You cannot afford so much," said one. "Yes, sir, I can," she answered.

On being pressed to explain, she said, "I am blind, and I said to my fellow strawworkers, 'How much money do you spend in a year for oil for your lamps when it is too dark to work nights?' They replied, 'Twenty-seven francs.' "

♦ ♦ ♦

The happiest people I have known are those consumed with desire to radiate happiness, to live unselfishly, to do everything within their power to help others. Selfishness scuttles happiness.
—B.C. Forbes

♦ ♦ ♦

Two little boys were overheard by a nurse in a children's ward discussing their hospital experiences.

Said one: "Are you medical or surgical?"

The other shook his head. "I don't know what you mean," he said.

The first little boy looked scornfully at his friend. He had been a patient in the ward for many weeks.

"Were you sick when you came," he persisted, "or did they make you sick after you came?" —*American Legion*

♦ ♦ ♦

The world's best safety device is located an inch or two above the eyebrows.

♦ ♦ ♦

Those who deny freedom to others deserve it not for themselves, and, under a just God, cannot long retain it.
—Abraham Lincoln

21

I sent my Soul through the Invisible
Some letter of that After-life to spell;
And by and by my Soul returned to me,
And answered, "I Myself am Heaven and Hell."
                    —from The Rubáiyát of Omar Khayyám

♦ ♦ ♦

Out of this nettle, danger, we pluck this flower, safety.
                              —William Shakespeare

♦ ♦ ♦

Sadness hears the clock strike every hour,
Happiness forgets the day of the month.   —Seneca

♦ ♦ ♦

I am not afraid of tomorrow. I have seen yesterday and I love
today.   —William Allen White

♦ ♦ ♦

I place economy among the first and most important virtues,
and public debt as the greatest of dangers. We must make our
choice between economy and liberty, or profusion and servitude.
                              —Thomas Jefferson

♦ ♦ ♦

You can unlock a man's whole life if you watch what words he
uses most.   —William Drummond

♦ ♦ ♦

The habit of looking at the best side of any event is worth more
than a thousand pounds a year.   —Samuel Johnson

22

God grant that not only the love of liberty, but a thorough knowledge of the rights of man may pervade all nations of the earth, so that a philosopher may set his foot anywhere on its surface, and say, "This is MY country."   —Benjamin Franklin

◆ ◆ ◆

Bad officials are elected by good people who do not vote.

◆ ◆ ◆

Truth is an excellent thing, but before one tells it one should be quite sure that one does so for the advantage of the person who hears it rather than for one's own self-satisfaction.
—W. Somerset Maugham

◆ ◆ ◆

Prosperity doth bewitch men, seeming clear,
But seas do laugh, show white, when rocks are near.
—John Webster

◆ ◆ ◆

Committee: a group which succeeds in getting something done only when it consists of three members, one of whom happens to be sick and another absent.   —Attributed to H.W. Van Loon

◆ ◆ ◆

Heat not a furnace for your foe so hot
That it do singe yourself.   —William Shakespeare

◆ ◆ ◆

A modern paradox—Hitler, the vegetarian, the teetotaler.

The comfort of having a friend may be taken away, but not that of having had one.

—Seneca

♦ ♦ ♦

Time is

Too slow for those who Wait,
Too swift for those who Fear,
Too long for those who Grieve,
Too short for those who Rejoice,
But for those who Love
    Time is not.

—Henry Van Dyke

♦ ♦ ♦

Our doubts are traitors,
And make us lose the good we oft might win,
By fearing to attempt.

—William Shakespeare

♦ ♦ ♦

There is no lovelier way to thank God for your sight, than by giving a helping hand to someone in the dark.　　—Helen Keller

♦ ♦ ♦

From a tombstone in Essex, England, 500 years old, is taken the following remarkable prediction:

"When pictures look alive with movements free,
    When ships like fishes swim below the sea,
When men outstripping birds can scan the sky,
    Then half the world sore drenched in blood shall lie."

♦ ♦ ♦

Silence is one of the great arts of conversation.

I do the very best I know how; the very best I can; and I mean to keep doing so until the end. If the end brings me out all right, what is said against me won't amount to anything. If the end brings me out wrong, ten angels swearing I was right would make no difference. —Abraham Lincoln

♦ ♦ ♦

Decision is a sharp knife that cuts clean and straight; indecision, a dull one that hacks and tears and leaves ragged edges behind it. —Gordon Graham

♦ ♦ ♦

If a man empties his purse into his head, no one can take it away from him. An investment in knowledge always pays the best interest. —Benjamin Franklin

♦ ♦ ♦

You gotta be a man to play baseball for a living but you gotta have a lot of little boy in you too. —Roy Campanella

♦ ♦ ♦

When Balzac's uncle died and left him a substantial legacy, Balzac wrote to a friend: "Yesterday at five in the morning, my uncle and I passed on to a better life."

♦ ♦ ♦

Chief Engineer: "So you want to become my son-in-law?"
Fireman: "No, I don't. But if I marry your daughter, I don't see how I can get out of it."

If I had a little bit of humility, I'd be perfect.   —Ted Turner

♦ ♦ ♦

The faster he talked of his honor
The faster we counted our spoons.   —Ralph Waldo Emerson

♦ ♦ ♦

He who is of a calm and happy nature will hardly feel the pressure of age, but to him who is of an opposite disposition youth and age are equally a burden.   —Plato

♦ ♦ ♦

When a fool has made up his mind the market has gone by.
     —Spanish Proverb

♦ ♦ ♦

A man cannot be too careful in the choice of his enemies.
     —Oscar Wilde

♦ ♦ ♦

When I am dead, I hope it may be said:
"His sins were scarlet, but his books were read."
     —Hilaire Belloc, who died in 1953

♦ ♦ ♦

A Jew's religious obsession is not to attain salvation but to make this a better world.   —Rabbi Myer S. Kripke

♦ ♦ ♦

The best doctors in the world are Doctor Diet, Doctor Quiet, and Doctor Merryman.   —Jonathan Swift

26

Write a letter to the author whose story gave you that delightful half hour last night. Write a letter to the cartoonist whose serial strip you avidly devoured this morning; to the teacher who inspired you twenty years ago; to the doctor who saved your baby's life; to your old employer to show him there was something more between you than a paycheck. Be a human being—write a letter.

There's a man in public life you admire, believe in, rave about. Write him a letter of praise, of encouragement. To be "with him in spirit" is not enough—show your spirit with a letter. We can't all be pioneers, crusaders, presidents—but we can help those brave men stay on the track and push through to a grand and glorious success if all we ever say is "Attaboy!" Write an "Attaboy" letter!

—James Mangan

♦ ♦ ♦

If you would lift me you must be on higher ground.

—Ralph Waldo Emerson

♦ ♦ ♦

Beware of little expenses; a small leak will sink a great ship.

—Benjamin Franklin

Following are two epitaphs of outlaws of Tombstone's pioneer days:

George Johnson—Hanged by mistake.

Lester Moore—
    Here lies Lester Moore
    Four slugs from a 44.
    No Les, no more.

To keep young, every day read a poem, hear a choice piece of music, view a fine painting, and, if possible, do a good action. Man's highest merit always is, as much as possible, to rule external circumstances, and as little as possible to let himself be ruled by them. —Johann Wolfgang von Goethe

◆ ◆ ◆

THE CHILDREN AND THE TREES

They've cut our three big maples down
   And left, where green boughs used to sigh
And sing beneath their leafy crown,
   A lonely hollow in the sky.

There is no swing, there is no shade,
   No dance of green leaves in the breeze,
No checkered sunlight where we played
   Before they took away our trees.

It's left a big hole in the blue
   And no birds sing the livelong day:
Oh, Earth must know an ache or two
   When kind old trees have gone away.   —Arthur Stringer

◆ ◆ ◆

Sign seen on a church: "Avoid the Easter rush—attend church this Sunday." —Paul Harvey

◆ ◆ ◆

After accepting an invitation to a dinner party, Mark Twain learned that he was to be the thirteenth at the table.
"Don't go," cautioned a superstitious friend. "It's bad luck."
"Nonsense," scoffed Twain.
The day after the dinner, he met his friend again.
"You were right. It was bad luck," said Twain. "There was only food enough for twelve."

Flower in the crannied wall,
I pluck you out of the crannies,
I hold you here, root and all, in my hand,
Little flower—but if I could understand
What you are, root and all, and all in all,
I should know what God and man is.

—Alfred, Lord Tennyson

♦ ♦ ♦

The children now love luxury, they have bad manners, contempt for authority, they show disrespect for elders and love chatter in place of exercise. They no longer rise when elders enter the room. They contradict their parents, chatter before company, gobble up dainties at the table, cross their legs, and tyrannize over their teachers. —Socrates

♦ ♦ ♦

When a little girl plays with dolls it's normal and healthy. When a big man does it's normal too—and dangerous.

♦ ♦ ♦

A wife helps a man more than anyone else; she criticizes him more. —Henry Ford

♦ ♦ ♦

A good listener is not only popular everywhere, but after a while he knows something. —Wilson Mizner

♦ ♦ ♦

And now, among the fading embers, these in the main are my regrets: when I am right, no one remembers; when I am wrong, no one forgets.

Edward Bok, the well-remembered magazine publisher, was a Hollander by birth, and naturally was fond of flowers. On one occasion he had thousands of crocuses planted outside the fence of his home.

"It's useless to plant your flowers beyond the fence," warned a passerby; "people will steal them."

Bok made no response. The next morning he nailed a sign on the fence: "These flowers are under the protection of the public." Not a blossom was ever taken.

◆ ◆ ◆

If you think North Americans are a vigorous people who love to exert themselves physically, are not afraid of work no matter how hard, just watch the natives in the business center of any United States town. They'd rather park illegally, pay a fine, or go to jail than leave their cars two blocks away and walk to their destination.
—Armando S. Pires, "The Natives Are Friendly"

◆ ◆ ◆

Remember Irvin Cobb's classic remark: "No speech can be entirely bad if it is short enough."

◆ ◆ ◆

A newspaper in New England recently published this announcement: "In case you find mistakes in this paper, please consider they were put there for a purpose. We publish something for everyone, and some folks are always looking for mistakes."

◆ ◆ ◆

They who give have all things; they who withhold have nothing.
—Hindu Proverb

Cowards die many times before their deaths;
The valiant never taste of death but once.
Of all the wonders that I yet have heard,
It seems to me most strange that men should fear;
Seeing that death, a necessary end,
Will come when it will come.   —William Shakespeare

♦ ♦ ♦

Vernon: "Grandma, if I was invited out to dinner somewhere, should I eat my pie with a fork?"
Grandma: "Certainly, Vernon."
Vernon: "You haven't got a piece of pie around the house that I could practice on, have you, Grandma?"

♦ ♦ ♦

SECRETARIAL HISTORY

Seems the Swiss publication, *Weltwoche,* of Zurich, got hold of a businessman's confidential budget record and, unsentimental folk that they are, published this transcript:

April

1	Ad for a secretary	10.00 francs
3	Violets	2.50 francs
4	Pralines	6.00 francs
8	Secretary's pay for week	120.00 francs
10	Flowers	12.00 francs
11	Pralines for my wife	18.00 francs
15	Secretary's pay for week	160.00 francs
18	Purse	70.00 francs
22	Gloria's pay for week	240.00 francs
24	Dinner and theatre with Gloria	190.00 francs
25	Candy for my wife	1.50 francs
28	Fur coat for wife	5600.00 francs
29	Ad for secretary	10.00 francs

♦ ♦ ♦

The best way to remember your wife's birthday is to forget it once.

To withhold deserved praise lest it should make its object conceited is as dishonest as to withhold payment of a just debt lest your creditor should spend the money badly.

—George Bernard Shaw

♦ ♦ ♦

How many cowards, whose hearts are all as false
As stairs of sand, wear yet upon their chins
The beards of Hercules and frowning Mars,
Who, inward searched, have livers as white as milk.
There is no voice so simple but assumes
Some mark of virtue on its outward parts.

—William Shakespeare

♦ ♦ ♦

The important thing is poise. How a man handles a situation is a much more important thing than the situation itself. Poise in all things and at all times. So few men have it.   —Lord Northcliffe

♦ ♦ ♦

"Great Spirit, help me to never judge another until I have walked two weeks in his moccasins!"

—Prayer of the Sioux Indians

♦ ♦ ♦

What is prudence in the conduct of every private family can scarce be folly in that of a great kingdom.   —Adam Smith

♦ ♦ ♦

Hard work will not kill a man, but it almost scares some men to death.

♦ ♦ ♦

In a society of free men, the proper aim of education is to prepare the individual to make wise decisions. All else is but contributory.   —Paul Woodring

EPITAPH ON HIMSELF

The body of Benjamin Franklin, Printer (like the cover of an old book, its contents torn out and stripped of its lettering and gilding), lies here, food for worms; but the work shall not be lost, for it will (as he believed) appear once more in a new and more elegant edition, revised and corrected by the author.

—Benjamin Franklin

♦ ♦ ♦

Even the lion has to defend himself against flies.

—German Proverb

♦ ♦ ♦

If you expect to save at all,
Do it while your salary's small.

♦ ♦ ♦

The man who first invented the art of supporting beggars made many wretched. —Menander, 300 B.C.

♦ ♦ ♦

He who has truth at his heart need never fear the want of persuasion on his tongue. —John Ruskin

♦ ♦ ♦

Avoid greatness; in a cottage there may be more real happiness than kings or their favorites enjoy. —Horace

♦ ♦ ♦

If it weren't for the last minute, a lot of things would never get done.

♦ ♦ ♦

Everything in the world may be endured except continual prosperity.

Mark Twain's habit of swearing was revolting to his wife, who tried her best to cure him of it. One day while shaving he cut himself. He cited his entire vocabulary and when he was finished, his wife repeated every word he had said. Mark Twain stunned her by saying calmly: "You have the words, dear, but you lack the tune."

◆ ◆ ◆

One of the things we have to be thankful for is that we don't get as much government as we pay for.
                    —Sometimes attributed to Charles F. Kettering

◆ ◆ ◆

Bad times have a scientific value. . . . We learn geology the morning after the earthquake.   —Ralph Waldo Emerson

◆ ◆ ◆

To be thrown upon one's own resources is to be cast into the very lap of fortune.   —Benjamin Franklin

◆ ◆ ◆

The young man who wants to marry happily should pick out a good mother and marry one of her daughters—any one.
                    —J. Ogden Armour

◆ ◆ ◆

It may be that the race is not always to the swift, nor the battle to the strong—but that's the way to bet.   —Damon Runyon

◆ ◆ ◆

The only gift is a portion of thyself.   —Ralph Waldo Emerson

◆ ◆ ◆

We think up clever repartee
Right after we're a departee.   —Jack Herbert

When the examination was over, the teacher in a mountain school told her pupils to write a pledge that they had neither received nor given help. One gangling youth, who had squirmed in dismay and mopped a bewildered brow throughout the ordeal, wrote: "I ain't received no help in this matter, and God knows I couldn't have gave any."

♦ ♦ ♦

The photographer had just taken a picture of a man on his ninety-ninth birthday. He thanked the old gentleman, saying, "I hope I'll be around to take your picture when you're a hundred." The old man replied, "Why not? You look pretty healthy."

♦ ♦ ♦

The strongest evidence to prove that God exists is a beautiful woman. —Giovanni Leone

♦ ♦ ♦

Some people have made an art of being slow to pick up the check. You've really got to hand it to them.

♦ ♦ ♦

Common sense is not sense common to everyone; but sense in common things. —William James

♦ ♦ ♦

He who first praises a book becomingly is next in merit to the author. —Walter S. Landor

♦ ♦ ♦

When I get sick, if "there's a lot of it going around," I don't feel quite as bad. —Beryl Pfizer

Shakespeare, in his day, was called "an upstart crow." Dryden said he wrote "below the dullest writers of our age." Pepys said that "Romeo and Juliet" was the worst play he had ever heard. Hume called him "a misshapen giant." Voltaire called him "a drunken savage." Goldsmith declared him "absurd." Byron sneered at him. Cheer up.

♦ ♦ ♦

I would rather appreciate the things I do not have than to have things I do not appreciate.

♦ ♦ ♦

Yes, the brutalities of progress are called revolutions. When they are over this is recognized: that the human race has been harshly treated, but that it has advanced.　　—Victor Hugo

♦ ♦ ♦

Fashion is a form of ugliness so intolerable that we have to alter it every six months.　　—Oscar Wilde

♦ ♦ ♦

The liar's punishment is not in the least that he is not believed, but that he cannot believe anyone else.　—George Bernard Shaw

♦ ♦ ♦

The injuries we do and those we suffer are seldom weighed on the same scales.　　—Aesop's Fables

It's foolish to worry about confused, miserable teenagers. Give them a few years and they'll turn out to be normal, miserable adults. —*Empire Magazine*

◆ ◆ ◆

Reading a book by Scott or Dickens after wading through a modern novel is like strolling through a sweet old garden after a visit to the glue works.

◆ ◆ ◆

Any government, like any family, can for a year spend a little more than it earns. But you and I know that continuance of that habit means the poorhouse. —Franklin D. Roosevelt

◆ ◆ ◆

It's funny that women aren't embarrassed when they buy men's pajamas, but a guy purchasing a nightgown acts as though he was making a deal with a dope peddler.

◆ ◆ ◆

What is a skeleton?
A skeleton is a person with the inside out and the outside off.

◆ ◆ ◆

Who owes no debt of crust or crumb can sleep within a beaten drum. —Chinese Proverb

◆ ◆ ◆

A Dublin doctor sent in a bill to a lady as follows: "To curing your husband till he died."

Yesterday is but a dream
And Tomorrow is only a vision,
  But Today,
Well-lived, makes every Yesterday
  A dream of happiness
And every Tomorrow a vision of Hope.
  Look well, therefore, to the Day.
Such is the salutation of the Dawn.   —Sanskrit

♦ ♦ ♦

Taxes are indeed very heavy and if those laid on by the Government were the only ones we had to pay we might the more easily discharge them—but:

We are taxed twice as much by our Idleness, three times as much by our Pride, four times as much by our Folly.
                                                —Benjamin Franklin

♦ ♦ ♦

We are always complaining that our days are few, and acting as though there would be no end of them.   —Seneca

♦ ♦ ♦

Thomas Jefferson once said:
"I served with General Washington in the Legislature of Virginia . . . and . . . with Doctor Franklin in Congress. I never heard either of them speak ten minutes at a time, nor to any but the main point."

♦ ♦ ♦

Pleasure is the last resort of the desperate. Happy people do not need to be amused.   —Thomas Carlyle

♦ ♦ ♦

Time is an herb that cures all diseases.   —Benjamin Franklin

38

Hie upon Hielands,
   and low upon Tay,
Bonnie George Campbell
   rade out on a day.

Saddled and bridled
   and gallant rade he;
Hame cam his guid horse,
   but never cam he.

Out cam his auld mither
   greeting fu' sair,
And out cam his bonnie bride
   riving her hair.

Saddled and bridled
   and booted rade he;
Toom hame cam the saddle,
   but never cam he.

"My meadow lies green,
   and my corn is unshorn,
My barn is to big,
   and my babe is unborn."

Saddled and bridled
   and booted rade he;
Toom hame cam the saddle,
   but never cam he.

—Thomas Percy

♦ ♦ ♦

The people sensible enough to give good advice are usually sensible enough to give none.　　　　　—Eden Phillpotts

♦ ♦ ♦

An expert is a man who makes his mistakes quietly.

♦ ♦ ♦

It takes less effort to keep an old customer satisfied than to get a new customer interested.

"It is a gloomy moment in history. Not in the lifetime of any man who reads this paper has there been so much grave and deep apprehension. Never has the future seemed so dark and incalculable. In France, the political cauldron seethes and bubbles with uncertainty. England and the British Empire are being sorely tried and exhausted in a social and economic struggle. The United States is beset with racial, industrial, and commercial chaos, drifting we know not where. Russia hangs like a storm cloud on the horizon of Europe—dark, menacing, and foreboding."

—*Harper's,* October, 1847

♦ ♦ ♦

He who has a why to live can bear with almost any how.

—Friedrich Wilhelm Nietzsche

♦ ♦ ♦

Our revels now are ended. These our actors,
As I foretold you, were all spirits and
Are melted into air, into thin air;
And, like the baseless fabric of this vision,
The cloud-capped towers, the gorgeous palaces,
The solemn temples, the great globe itself,
Yea, all which it inherit, shall dissolve;
And, like this insubstantial pageant faded,
Leave not a rack behind. We are such stuff
As dreams are made on, and our little life
Is rounded with a sleep.   —William Shakespeare

♦ ♦ ♦

Keep thy shop and thy shop will keep thee.
Light gains make heavy purses.   —George Chapman

Sweet and low, sweet and low,
Wind of the western sea,
Low, low, breathe and blow,
Wind of the western sea!
Over the rolling waters go,
Come from the dying moon, and blow,
Blow him again to me;
While my little one, while my pretty one, sleeps.

Sleep and rest, sleep and rest,
Father will come to thee soon;
Rest, rest, on mother's breast,
Father will come to thee soon;
Father will come to his babe in the nest,
Silver sails all out of the west
Under the silver moon:
Sleep, my little one, sleep, my pretty one, sleep.
—Alfred, Lord Tennyson

♦ ♦ ♦

Fretting about things you cannot do anything about creates more frustration than any other single factor. I believe that it can be a forerunner and a contributor to ulcers, high blood pressure, and similar disorders. . . . If you try to reason with things you cannot do anything about, you are lost. Save your energy and your sanity by doing something on those matters that have an answer.
—Ralph W. O'Farrell

♦ ♦ ♦

Money isn't everything, but it's way ahead of whatever is in second place.
—Gordon Gammack

♦ ♦ ♦

Great works are performed not by strength but by perseverance.
—Samuel Johnson

Question in a memorandum received by the Hampshire (England) Fire Service: "How many people do you employ, broken down by sex?"

♦ ♦ ♦

A third-grader came home from school recently and announced jubilantly that his class had a substitute teacher. "And she has only two rules we have to follow," he said, "sit down and shut up."
—Mack McGinnis

♦ ♦ ♦

The Texas oil man's daughter returned from college and he was showing her around their new mansion. They stopped at the swimming pool to watch several athletic young men cavorting on the diving board. "Oh, daddy," she exclaimed, "you've stocked it for me."

♦ ♦ ♦

When the little girl returned home from her first day at school, her father asked her what she had done.
"I did what all the other children did," said the little girl.
"That's good," smiled her father proudly. "What was it that you all did?"
"We cried," said the little girl.

♦ ♦ ♦

The skipper of a sinking pleasure boat out of Chesapeake Bay radioed repeatedly for help. "We're on our way," the Coast Guard replied. "What is your position? Repeat. What is your position?"
"I'm executive vice president of the First National Bank," answered the yachtsman. "Please hurry."

A life of ease is a difficult pursuit.   —William Cowper

♦ ♦ ♦

The greatest remedy for anger is delay.   —Seneca

♦ ♦ ♦

Always do right. This will gratify some people, and astonish the rest.   —Mark Twain

♦ ♦ ♦

Prayer, like radium, is a luminous and self-generating form of energy.   —Dr. Alexis Carrel

♦ ♦ ♦

One of the most durable satisfactions in life is to lose oneself in one's work.   —Harry Emerson Fosdick

♦ ♦ ♦

After Carl Sandburg's six volumes of Lincoln were published, someone once commented in his presence that the book was "so very American."

"Yes," Sandburg agreed. "It's a book about a man whose mother could not sign her name, written by a man whose father could not sign his. Perhaps that could happen only in America."

♦ ♦ ♦

Michael Faraday, father of our electrical age, was giving a demonstration before the British Royal Scientific Society of London. A rising young politician of the day, William Gladstone, was present. He evinced polite interest at first and then became bored, saying, "It's all very interesting, Mr. Faraday, but what in God's earth good is it?"

"Some day," answered Faraday, "you politicians will be able to tax it!"

Without freedom of thought, there can be no such thing as wisdom; and no such thing as public liberty without freedom of speech; which is the right of every man as far as by it he does not hurt or control the right of another; and this is the only check it ought to suffer and the only bounds it ought to know. . . . Whoever would overthrow the liberty of a nation must begin by subduing the freedom of speech, a thing terrible to traitors.

—Benjamin Franklin

◆ ◆ ◆

A famous doctor was asked recently to name the most devastating disease today. "Loneliness," he said. "Just plain loneliness." He went on, "The longer I practice, the surer I am that there's no condition so acute, so universal. Everybody, at one time or another, is subject to its ravages. With many the disease becomes chronic. And not a few live constantly under its blight—melancholy, bored, forlorn, friendless. Doctors can't cure it. Only the victims can."

—Clarence W. Hall

◆ ◆ ◆

A preacher who recently announced that there are 726 sins, has been besieged for copies of the list.

◆ ◆ ◆

Doctor: "I don't like the looks of your husband."
Wife: "I don't either, but he's good to the children."

◆ ◆ ◆

No man can believe in the brotherhood of man and be comfortable . . . It is a doctrine that takes away all of our cushions and leaves us with a cross.   —Studdert-Kennedy, English Minister

44

Never a tear bedims the eye
That time and patience will not dry.　　　　—Bret Harte

◆ ◆ ◆

Happiness sneaks in through a door you didn't know you left open.　　　　—John Barrymore

◆ ◆ ◆

He will always be a slave who does not know how to live upon a little.　　　　—Horace

◆ ◆ ◆

The way to gain a good reputation is to endeavor to be what you desire to appear.　　　　—Socrates

◆ ◆ ◆

Ideas are the mightiest influence on earth. One great thought breathed into a man may regenerate him. —William E. Channing

◆ ◆ ◆

How desperately difficult it is to be honest with oneself. It is much easier to be honest with other people.　—Edward F. Benson

◆ ◆ ◆

Ring Lardner attended an annual homecoming game in the days when Illinois boasted the galloping Red Grange and a crack student battery of artillery. Just before game time, the first salute gun was fired as Governor Small entered his box. Lardner jumped from his seat, and demanded, "What was that?" "For the governor," was the answer. Just then the second gun blasted away. "My God!" cried Lardner. "They missed him."

◆ ◆ ◆

I never knew an auctioneer to lie, unless it was absolutely necessary.　　　　—John Billings

The nearest thing to a drumbeat is the repetition of the name of the sponsor's product on radio and TV. I have heard an adcaster repeat a name, address, and telephone number, three times after I thought he was out of breath.

—William Feather

♦ ♦ ♦

The worst bankrupt in the world is the man who has lost his enthusiasm. Let a man lose everything else in the world but his enthusiasm and he will come through again to success.

—H.W. Arnold

♦ ♦ ♦

A faithful friend is the medicine of life.　　　—Ecclesiasticus

♦ ♦ ♦

It is much more important to be human than to be important.

—Will Rogers

♦ ♦ ♦

Husband: Hello, Dear—How did everything go today?
Wife: Oh, I had a little argument with the water department.
Husband: Who won?
Wife: Nobody—it was a tie. They don't get any money and we don't get any water.

♦ ♦ ♦

A meek little man in a restaurant timidly touched the arm of a man putting on a coat. "Excuse me," he said, "but do you happen to be Mr. Smith of Newcastle?"

"No, I'm not!" the man answered impatiently.

"Oh—er—well," stammered the first man, "you see, I am, and that's his overcoat you're putting on."

Tenant: Why do you raise my rent when my room is all the way up in the miserable attic?

Landlord: Because you use more stairs than anyone else.

♦ ♦ ♦

Two Ohio boys got lost driving through Tennessee. Along the deserted road trudged a native of whom they asked, "Which way to Chattanooga?" The man stared at them and then asked, "Where you boys from?"

"Ohio."

"I thought so," he said. "Wal, you found it in 1863. Let's see you find it again." —Carrie Dickenson

♦ ♦ ♦

It is a difficult and painful task to make a will because, for the first time, you realize that you are living on leased securities, and that you cannot take anything but your character with you.

—Dr. O.A. Battista

♦ ♦ ♦

Life is a fatal adventure. It can have only one end. So why not make it as far ranging and free as possible? —Alexander Eliot

♦ ♦ ♦

Many men owe the grandeur of their lives to their tremendous difficulties. —Spurgeon

♦ ♦ ♦

More persons, on the whole, are humbugged by believing in nothing, than by believing too much. —P.T. Barnum

47

A CHILD SPEAKS

Will people never, never learn,
    That meadows should be played in?
How long before they really know
    That streams were made to wade in?
They should be shown, and made to see
    That caves were made to talk in,
That trees were really made to climb,
    And rain is meant to walk in.
Instead, they build their houses tight,
    As though they're meant to stay in;
Will people never, never learn
    The world was meant to play in?
                —Barbara A. Jones

◆ ◆ ◆

The tongue is the deadliest of all blunt instruments.

◆ ◆ ◆

Some people believe everything you tell them—if you whisper it.

◆ ◆ ◆

Conceit is a queer disease; it makes everybody sick but the one who has it.

◆ ◆ ◆

When saving for old age, be sure to lay up a few pleasant thoughts.

◆ ◆ ◆

A bargain is something you cannot use at a price you cannot resist.

◆ ◆ ◆

Men at some time are masters of their fates:
The fault, dear Brutus, is not in our stars,
But in ourselves.   —William Shakespeare

A hypocritical Boston tycoon once told Mark Twain, "Before I die I mean to make a pilgrimage to the top of Mount Sinai in the Holy Land, and read the Ten Commandments aloud." "Why don't you stay right home in Boston," suggested Twain, "and keep them?"

♦ ♦ ♦

The only way to keep your health is to eat what you don't want, drink what you don't like, and do what you'd rather not.
—Mark Twain

♦ ♦ ♦

The punishment that the wise suffer who refuse to take part in the government is to live under the government of worse men.
—Plato

♦ ♦ ♦

There is a pleasure in being in a ship beaten about by a storm, when we are sure that it will not founder.   —Blaise Pascal

♦ ♦ ♦

I can see how a man can look down upon the earth and be an atheist, but I cannot conceive how he could look up into the heavens and say there is no God.   —Abraham Lincoln

♦ ♦ ♦

It is a great misfortune neither to have enough wit to talk well nor enough judgment to be silent.   —Jean de La Bruyère

♦ ♦ ♦

On converting an enemy into a friend: Rejoice—but don't relax.

When someone asks if there's someplace I'd rather be,
I feel comfortable anywhere as long as I'm with me.
I like myself, tho not in a narcissistic way,
I'm the only one who can get me through the day.
Pleasure comes from being with yourself,
And not from being someplace else.   —John Covert

♦ ♦ ♦

So plant as though you will live forever; so labor as though you
will die tomorrow.   —Mark Twain

♦ ♦ ♦

Over 40 percent of American women sleep in the nude, while
only 25 percent of the men do, say the authors of *The Sleep Book*.

♦ ♦ ♦

If you tell a good story, its narration will remind your hearers of
a bad one.   —Edgar Watson Howe

♦ ♦ ♦

Always look on the bright side of things; but if you are buying
them, it's well to look on both sides.

♦ ♦ ♦

Quiet minds cannot be perplexed or frightened but go on in
fortune or misfortune at their own private pace, like a clock
during a thunderstorm.   —Robert Louis Stevenson

♦ ♦ ♦

Forbidden fruit is responsible for many a bad jam.

I like tall girls, short girls, fat girls, skinny girls. I do prefer companions who are able to sing two-part harmony.

—George Burns

♦ ♦ ♦

She had a million dollar figure—then inflation set in.

—Arnold H. Glasow

♦ ♦ ♦

Tact is the fine art of not saying what you think.

—Franklin P. Jones

♦ ♦ ♦

Strew gladness on the paths of men—
You will not pass this way again.   —Sam Walter Foss

♦ ♦ ♦

Nothing is cheap which is superfluous, for what one does not need, is dear at a penny.   —Plutarch

♦ ♦ ♦

If a man does not make new acquaintances as he advances through life, he will soon find himself left alone. A man, sir, should keep his friendship in a constant repair. —Samuel Johnson

♦ ♦ ♦

A cruel story runs on wheels, and every hand oils the wheels as they run.   —George Eliot

♦ ♦ ♦

An oppressive government is more to be feared than a tiger.

—Confucius

♦ ♦ ♦

One man with courage makes a majority.   —Andrew Jackson

THE PROLOGUE TO THE CANTERBURY TALES

Whan that Aprille with his shoures sote
The droghte of Marche hath perced to the rote,
And bathed every veyne in swich licour,
Of which vertu engendred is the flour,
Whan Zephirus eek with his swete breeth
Inspired hath in every holt and heeth
The tendre croppes, and the yonge sonne
Hath in the Ram his halfe cours y-ronne,
And smale fowles maken melodye,
That slepen al the night with open yë,
(So priketh hem nature in hir corages):
Than longen folk to goon on pilgrimages
(And palmers for to seken straunge strondes)
To ferne halwes, couthe in sondry londes;
and specially, from every shires ende
Of Engelond to Caunterbury they wende,
the holy blisful martir for to seke
That hem hath holpen, whan that they were seke.
                                    —Geoffrey Chaucer

◆ ◆ ◆

I don't kno ov enny thing that would use the whole ov us up
more thoroughly, than tew hav all ov our wishes gratified.
                                    —Josh Billings

◆ ◆ ◆

Advice from an old carpenter: Measure twice and saw once.

◆ ◆ ◆

Used car salesman to prospect: "There isn't a dent in it because
it belonged to a little old lady whose little old husband wouldn't let
her drive it."

◆ ◆ ◆

The world expects results. Don't tell others about the labor
pains—show 'em the baby!   —Arnold H. Glasow

A gentleman lying on his death-bed was questioned by his inconsolable prospective widow. "Poor Mike," said she, "is there anythin' that wud make ye comfortable? Anythin' ye ask for I'll get for ye."

"Plase, Bridget," he responded, "I think I'd like a wee taste of the ham I smell a-boilin' in the kitchen."

"Arrah, go on," responded Bridget. "Divil a bit of that ham ye'll get. 'Tis for the wake."

♦ ♦ ♦

We can orbit the earth, we can touch the moon, but this society has not devised a way for two people to live together in harmony for seven straight days without wanting to strangle each other.

—George Leonard

♦ ♦ ♦

In the long run, the pessimist may be proved right, but the optimist has a better time on the trip.

♦ ♦ ♦

Out of the night that covers me,
Black as the Pit from pole to pole,
I thank whatever gods may be
For my unconquerable soul.

In the fell clutch of circumstance,
I have not winced nor cried aloud;
Under the bludgeonings of chance
My head is bloody, but unbowed.

Beyond this place of wrath and tears
Looms but the Horror of the shade,
And yet the menace of the years
Finds and shall find me unafraid.

It matters not how strait the gate,
How charged with punishment the scroll,
I am the master of my fate:
I am the captain of my soul.   —William Ernest Henley

Few men during their lifetime come anywhere near exhausting the resources dwelling within them. There are deep wells of strength that are never used. —Richard E. Byrd

♦ ♦ ♦

Age has nothing to do with learning a new way to be stupid. —J.C. Salak

♦ ♦ ♦

Among life's mysteries is the way something you read in yesterday's paper has disappeared when you try to find it again.

♦ ♦ ♦

Tell me how a people uses its leisure and I will tell you the quality of its civilization. —Maurice Maeterlinck

♦ ♦ ♦

A Public Person . . .

Once a man achieves a degree of notoriety in his chosen profession, he is going to become, to some degree, a public person. People are going to recognize him. At first it's a grand feeling. Man, there's nothing like it. But it wears thin after a while. It finally reaches a point where an athlete has to drive himself to make public appearances.

♦ ♦ ♦

Music is the only language in which you cannot say a mean or sarcastic thing. —John Erskine

♦ ♦ ♦

"Beauty is truth, truth beauty,"—that is all
Ye know on earth, and all ye need to know. —John Keats

No one can make you feel inferior without your consent.
                                                    —Eleanor Roosevelt

◆ ◆ ◆

How it improves people for us when we begin to love them.

◆ ◆ ◆

"Which way to Rock Ridge?" asked a motorist of a dejected looking man perched on a fence near a ramshackle farmhouse.

The native languidly waved his hand toward the right.

"Thanks," said the motorist. "How far is it?"

"Tain't so very far," was the drawling reply. "When you get there, you'll wish it was a durn sight farther."

◆ ◆ ◆

Some old-fashioned mothers who can remember their husband's first kiss now have daughters who can't remember their first husband.   —F.G. Kernan

◆ ◆ ◆

An extravagance is anything you buy that is of no earthly use to your spouse.

◆ ◆ ◆

One should start his life each day with a turning in of his life to the divine wave length that contacts the great universal power station from which comes illumination and divine guidance for your today.

We need God as our compass guide and not least God's protecting care each day in this mad speed reckless world. —R.V. Ewart

Too often the furniture which has been faithfully preserved from the marks of family life sells at an auction for a paltry sum.
—Marcelene Cox

♦ ♦ ♦

When you tell the truth you do not have to remember what you said.

♦ ♦ ♦

An officer in the Royal Navy being considered for promotion may submit a letter to the Admiralty concerning his fitness. Such a letter can invite attention to some talent previously unnoted in the official record, some past success previously unheralded, or attempt to cast a more favorable light on some aspect of his career that was not so successful. But, whatever its content, the tone of the letter is invariably formal, correct, and solemn. So when the following letter reached the Admiralty not long ago, it created quite a stir:

"As our Lordships are no doubt aware, there is always one name on every promotion list of whom everyone remarks, 'How on earth did he make it?' I wish Their Lordships to be assured that I shall not be the least bit discomfited if, upon publication of the next Commander list, I am that officer." P.S. He made it.

♦ ♦ ♦

This world belongs to the energetic.   —Ralph Waldo Emerson

♦ ♦ ♦

You can't hold a man down without staying down with him.
—Booker T. Washington

Errors, like straws, upon the surface flow;
He who would search for pearls must dive below. —John Dryden

♦ ♦ ♦

It takes less time to do a thing right than it does to explain why
you did it wrong. —Henry Wadsworth Longfellow

♦ ♦ ♦

The trouble with the world is that the stupid are cocksure and
the intelligent full of doubt. —Bertrand Russell, Earl Russell

♦ ♦ ♦

To be happy and contented—count your blessings—not your
cash.

♦ ♦ ♦

Listen, children:
Your father is dead.
From his old coats
I'll make you little jackets;
I'll make you little trousers
From his old pants.
There'll be in his pockets
Things he used to put there,
Keys and pennies
Covered with tobacco;
Dan shall have the pennies
To save in his bank;
Anne shall have the keys
To make a pretty noise with
Life must go on,
And the dead be forgotten;
Life must go on,
Though good men die;
Anne, eat your breakfast;
Dan, take your medicine;
Life must go on;
I forget just why.

—Edna St. Vincent Millay

SUMMER

The trouble with life, you're halfway through before you realize it's one of those do-it-yourself deals.

♦ ♦ ♦

The time to be nice to people is when you don't have to be.
—F.H. Beaumont

♦ ♦ ♦

You can always recognize a no-parking area. There are fewer cars there. —Franklin P. Jones

♦ ♦ ♦

The strongest bond of human sympathy, outside of the family relation, should be one uniting all working people, of all nations, and tongues, and kindreds. Nor should this lead us to a war upon property, or the owners of property. Property is the fruit of labor; property is desirable; is a positive good in the world. That some should be rich shows that others may become rich and, hence, is just encouragement to industry and enterprise. Let not him who is houseless pull down the house of another, but let him labor diligently and build one for himself, thus, by example, assuring that his own shall be safe from violence when built.
—Abraham Lincoln

♦ ♦ ♦

What a scarcity of news there would be if we all obeyed the Ten Commandments.

♦ ♦ ♦

The average woman of 35 isn't. —Franklin P. Jones

♦ ♦ ♦

The man who knows little is proud that he knows so much; the man who knows a lot is sorry that he knows so little.

60

Do you know the source of the marriage vows? Few do. The present wording of that marriage contract is not prescribed or specified by Holy Writ. It is nowhere to be found in the Bible. The framework for the words dates back to the primitive Sarum, an English rite in 1078. That formula evolved out of centuries of trial and error. Its workability is based on the experience of many generations—on honesty, as much as on morality. We have learned that this code for human conduct is best. —Paul Harvey

♦ ♦ ♦

Actually, although it is not common knowledge, there were five ships on Columbus's fleet when he sailed for the New World. Two of them went over the edge. —Marty Engels

♦ ♦ ♦

Hark! Hark! The Lark!

Hark! hark! the lark at heaven's gate sings,
    And Phoebus 'gins arise,
His steeds to water at those springs
On chaliced flowers that lies;
And winking Mary-buds begin
    To ope their golden eyes:
With everything that pretty is,
    My lady sweet, arise. —William Shakespeare

♦ ♦ ♦

The infinite sinuousness, nuance, and complexity of music enable it to speak in a thousand different accents to a thousand different listeners, and to say with non-commital and moving intimacy what no language would acknowledge or express and what no situations in life could completely exhaust or make possible. —Irwin Edman

No word in the English language carries more misleading meanings than love does. When we say a person loves tennis, loves Cokes, loves his car, loves Simon and Garfunkle, loves his wife, we may mean he is attached in some way to all of them, but beyond that the word becomes distorted beyond understanding. Both caring and hatred can be expressed by love. "I love you" can mean genuine affection or cruel domination, because who can protest something done "because I love you." As we use love, it can mean anything or nothing.

The Greeks had at least four words for love. First, there is epithemia, or sheer physical desire or lust. Second, there is eros. This suggests a passionate attraction to that which is good, true, and beautiful. It is a longing, a desire for what is worth possessing. Eros may include sex, but sex for the release of tension or for recreation only, is not eros. A third word is philia, which refers basically to friendship or brotherly love. It is comradely, warm, affectionate, but confined to those who are near and dear to you. Agapé is self-giving love that is not based primarily on emotion. It is action taken on behalf of others—friends and enemies. It is undertaken to foster the well-being and growth of the person loved.

Agapé is characteristic of God's action. Agapé is what Paul speaks of in his First Letter to the Corinthians: "Love is patient; love is kind and envies no one. Love is never boastful, nor conceited, nor rude; never selfish, not quick to take offense. Love keeps no score of wrongs; does not gloat over other men's sins, but delights in the truth. There is nothing love cannot face; there is no limit to its faith, its hope, and its endurance." —Roy W. Fairchild

♦ ♦ ♦

In words, as fashions, the same rule will hold;
Alike fantastic, if too new, or old.
Be not the first by whom the new are tried,
Nor yet the last to lay the old aside.   —Alexander Pope

A RED, RED ROSE

O, my Luve's like a red, red rose,
   That's newly sprung in June;
O, my luve's like the melodie
   That's sweetly play'd in tune.—
So fair art thou, my bonie lass,
   So deep in luve am I;
And I will luve thee still, my Dear,
   Till a' the seas gang dry.—
Till a' the seas gang dry, my Dear,
   And the rocks melt wi' the sun:
And I will luve thee still, my Dear,
   While the sands o' life shall run.—
And fare thee weel, my only Luve,
   And fare thee weel, a while!
And I will come again, my Luve,
   Tho' it were ten thousand mile!   —Robert Burns

◆ ◆ ◆

When you have a dream you've got to grab it and never let go.
        —Carol Burnett

◆ ◆ ◆

One of the many things nobody ever tells you about middle age is that it's such a nice change from being young.
        —Dorothy Canfield Fisher

◆ ◆ ◆

Few people have ever been truly free of possessions, but these few have left eternal impressions on the world. Jesus was one. Mahatma Gandhi was likely one, and Socrates another. Socrates understated it wittily. At an auction to which he went with a friend he looked around and then remarked, "It is wonderful how many things there are in the world that I do not need."

63

Courage leads starward, fear toward death.   —Seneca

♦ ♦ ♦

Casey Stengel, manager of the New York Mets and director of a Glendale, California, bank, described his duties as bank director to Al Lopez, Chicago White Sox manager and also a bank director, who repeated the description to Arthur Daley of *The New York Times:*
"There ain't nothin' to it. You go into the fancy meeting room and you just sit there and never open your yap. And long as you don't say nothin' they don't know whether you're smart or dumb. When the question of a loan comes up if it's a friend of yours you vote to give it to him and if he ain't a friend, you don't."

♦ ♦ ♦

Wouldst thou fashion for thyself a seemly life?
Then do not fret over what is past and gone;
And spite of all thou may'st have left behind
Live each day as if thy life were just begun.
                              —Johann Wolfgang von Goethe

♦ ♦ ♦

Learn to laugh—laugh is better than medicine.
Learn to attend to your own business. Few men can handle their own well.
Learn to tell a story. A well-told story is like a sunbeam in a sick room.
Learn to say kind things—nobody ever resents them.
Learn to avoid nasty remarks—they give neither the hearer nor the speaker any lasting satisfaction.
Learn to stop grumbling. If you can't see any good in the world keep the bad to yourself.
Learn to hide aches with a smile—nobody is interested anyway.
Learn to keep troubles to yourself—nobody wants to take them from you.
Above all, learn to smile. It pays.

In the summer of 1949 Albert Schweitzer came to America. He was greeted by a large group of friends in Grand Central Station, New York City. As he and his hosts walked through the station, he spied an elderly woman lugging her heavy traveling bags. Immediately he left his friends, went over and carried her bags for her to the taxicab.

♦ ♦ ♦

I've got insomnia so bad, doctor, I can't even sleep when it's time to get up!

♦ ♦ ♦

The difference between a conviction and a prejudice is that you can explain a conviction without getting angry.

♦ ♦ ♦

During World War II, a German soldier observed a French peasant looking down a deep hole and repeating to himself, "26-26-26-26." His curiosity aroused, the German approached the man and demanded to know what was going on. The peasant pointed at the hole and the soldier leaned over and peered down it. Whereupon the peasant pushed the soldier down the hole. A few minutes later, another German soldier spotted the peasant peering down a hole as he repeated to himself, "27-27-27-27."

—Jack Carter

♦ ♦ ♦

I think art is a great big river that just flows and it's been flowing for thousands of years. . . . Art doesn't win wars, but it's the only thing that remains after the civilizations go. Nobody knows much about the politics of certain Egyptian dynasties but people remember the art, the great things that were created.

—Robert Scull

Don't look back. Something may be gaining on you.

—Satchel Paige

♦ ♦ ♦

Want to stake a mining claim? It's easier than you think.

First, go find some federal land—there are more than 750 million acres of it, mostly in the West—and mark off the boundaries of the section you want. (Nobody knows how much of the 750 million acres remains unclaimed, because there's no central place where claims are recorded.) Under the 1872 mining law, you're supposed to have found a valuable mineral, but at this stage you don't have to prove it.

After meeting some minor conditions imposed by most states, the federal law requires only two things: That you do some so-called assessment work each year and that you be prepared to prove your claim is valid if it is challenged.

If you want full title, you can apply for a "patent"; there isn't any requirement, however, that you seek the patent. If you do seek it, you must prove there are minerals on the land and pay $2.50 an acre. This is the first time that you must make your presence on the land known to the federal government. Once the government issues a patent, you don't have to mine the land. Under the law, it's yours—and you can do anything you want with it.

♦ ♦ ♦

I pity the creature who doesn't work, at whichever end of the social scale he may regard himself as being.

—Theodore Roosevelt

♦ ♦ ♦

"I am hurt," Sir Andrew Barton said,
"I am hurt, but I am not slain;
I'll lie me down and bleed a while,
And then I'll fight again."

—Old Scotch Ballad

66

So the story goes, when Captain Cook discovered Australia, his sailors brought a strange animal aboard ship whose name they didn't know. Cook sent a sailor ashore to inquire of the natives the name of this creature. He returned and reported it was known as a "kangaroo."

Many years passed before it was learned that when the natives were asked the name of the animal and replied, "kangaroo," they were simply asking, "What did you say?"

◆ ◆ ◆

One can never pay in gratitude; one can only pay "in kind" somewhere else in life.   —Anne Morrow Lindbergh

◆ ◆ ◆

I met Thomas Edison and Alexander Graham Bell, and many others who impressed me as great people, but pride in them and their achievements has not over-awed me, for I am not convinced that the comforts and advancements which they brought into the world have made people more content and happy than the Indians were through the centuries on the mountains, prairies, and deserts of the primeval, virgin continent.   —Chief Red Fox

◆ ◆ ◆

There is one thing stronger than all the armies in the world, and that is an Idea whose time has come.   —Victor Hugo

◆ ◆ ◆

"Robert," said the earnest social worker to the village reprobate, "the last time I met you, you made me very happy because you were sober. Today you have made me unhappy because you are intoxicated." "Yes," replied Robert with a beaming smile. "Today's my turn to be happy."

Don't, like the cat, try to get more out of an experience than there is in it. The cat, having sat upon a hot stove lid, will not sit upon a hot stove lid again. Nor upon a cold stove lid. —Mark Twain

♦ ♦ ♦

Hast thou named all the birds without a gun?
Loved the wood-rose, and left it on its stalk?
At rich men's tables eaten bread and pulse?
Unarmed, faced danger with a heart of trust?
And loved so well a high behavior,
In man or maid, that thou from speech refrained,
Nobility, more nobly to repay?
O, be my friend, and teach me to be thine!
—Ralph Waldo Emerson

♦ ♦ ♦

A wrong inflicted deliberately is certain to come back to thee.
—Alisher Navoi

♦ ♦ ♦

Don't care for cocktail parties. Don't care much for giving them. Everyone comes in and has drinks, and then they go away and say what a lousy party. Some people love parties, I don't see much in them. As far as I am concerned, you get buttonholed by one individual in the corner of the room and you can't get away, that is my experience of parties. I'd rather be at home, reading a book. —Alfred Hitchcock

The Roman philosopher and statesman, Cicero, said this some 2,000 years ago, and it is still true today. The six mistakes of man are:

1. The delusion that personal gain is made by crushing others.
2. The tendency to worry about things that cannot be changed or corrected.
3. Insisting that a thing is impossible because we cannot accomplish it.
4. Refusing to set aside trivial preferences.
5. Neglecting development and refinement of the mind, and not acquiring the habit of reading and study.
6. Attempting to compel other persons to believe and live as we do.

♦ ♦ ♦

He who has nine things but lacks one is poor if he dwells on the one, while he who has one thing but lacks nine is rich unless he dwells on the nine.   —John Andrew Holmes

♦ ♦ ♦

Whatsoever things are true, whatsoever things are honorable, whatsoever things are just, whatsoever things are pure, whatsoever things are lovely, whatsoever things are of good report; if there be any virtue, and if there be any praise, think on these things.
                              —St. Paul in letter to Philippians

♦ ♦ ♦

Fog . . .

The fog comes
on little cat feet.
It sits looking
over the harbor and city
on silent haunches
and then moves on.   —Carl Sandburg

We hold these Truths to be self-evident, that all Men are created equal, that they are endowed by their Creator with certain un-alienable Rights, that among these are Life, Liberty and the Pursuit of Happiness—that to secure these Rights, Governments are instituted among Men, deriving their just Powers from the Consent of the Governed, that whenever any Form of Government becomes destructive of these Ends, it is the Right of the People to alter or to Abolish it, and to institute new Government, laying its foundation on such Principles, and organizing its Powers in such Form, as to them shall seem most likely to effect their Safety and Happiness.   —Declaration of Independence

◆ ◆ ◆

Before borrowing money from a friend, decide which you need most.   —W.A. Clarke

◆ ◆ ◆

In getting ready to face the public with the beginning of a new day, be sure to consider your attitude. Your attitude will have a greater influence on you and the people you meet than the clothes you wear or the way you comb your hair or fix your face.
                                        —Erwin L. McDonald

◆ ◆ ◆

Checking Up . . .
    (From the *Omaha World Herald,* July 20, 1971)
    Question: Who said, "High heels were invented by a woman who had been kissed on the forehead?"
    Answer: That was Christopher Morley. He also said:
1. "No man is lonely while eating spaghetti."
2. "Few girls are as well-shaped as a good horse."
3. "A human being is an ingenious assembly of portable plumb-ing."
4. "Life is a foreign language: All men mispronounce it."
✳5. "There's so much to say, but your eyes keep interrupting me."

70

Never, I say, had a country so many openings to happiness as this. . . . Her cause was good. Her principles just and liberal. Her temper serene and firm. . . . The remembrance then of what is past, if it operates rightly must inspire her with the most laudable of an ambition, that of adding to the fair fame she began with.

The world has seen her great adversity. . . . Let then, the world see that she can bear prosperity; and that her honest virtue in time of peace is equal to the bravest virtue in time of war.

—Thomas Paine

◆ ◆ ◆

The world is full of cactus, but we don't have to sit on it.　　—Will Foley

◆ ◆ ◆

Habit is a cable; we weave a thread of it each day, and at last we cannot break it.　　—Horace Mann

◆ ◆ ◆

It is a socialist idea that making profits is a vice. I consider the real vice is making losses.　　—Winston Churchill

◆ ◆ ◆

A man there was and they called him mad; the more he gave the more he had.　　—John Bunyan

◆ ◆ ◆

A larger than average woman stepped on the scales, not knowing they were out of order. The indicator stopped at 75 pounds.

A little boy standing by watched her intently. "Whaddaya know," he marveled. "She's hollow!"

◆ ◆ ◆

When a man seeks your advice, he generally wants your praise.
—G.K. Chesterton

With malice toward none, with charity for all; with firmness in the right as God gives us to see the right, let us strive on to finish the work we are in, to bind up the nation's wounds, to care for him who shall have borne the battle, and for his widow and his orphan, to do all which may achieve and cherish a just and lasting peace among ourselves and with all nations.   —Abraham Lincoln

The late columnist, Arthur Brisbane, declined to accept William Randolph Hearst's offer of a six-months' paid vacation in appreciation of his excellent work.

"There are two reasons why I will not accept your generous offer, Mr. Hearst," said the famous editor. "The first is that if I quit writing my column for half a year, it might affect the circulation of your newspaper. The second reason is that it might not!"

Think twice; do once.

The word "Yankee" implies different things to different people. To foreigners, a Yankee is an American. To an American a Yankee is a Northerner. To a Northerner a Yankee is a New Englander. To a New Englander a Yankee is a Vermonter. To a Vermonter a Yankee is a person who eats pie for breakfast.

To marry a second time represents the triumph of hope over experience. —Samuel Johnson

♦ ♦ ♦

When two people are under the influence of the most violent, most insane, most delusive, and most transient of passions, they are required to swear that they will remain in that excited, abnormal, and exhausting condition continuously until death do them part. —George Bernard Shaw

♦ ♦ ♦

A man who works with his hands is a laborer. A man who works with his hands and his brains is a craftsman. But a man who works with his brains and the hands of others is an executive.

♦ ♦ ♦

Gossip . . .

The world is full of gossip,
You can find it on the street,
In the office or the parlor,
Any place where people meet.

Since gossip is but idle chat,
We could do away with that,
But what a calamity it would be
To a cocktail party or a tea.

Most folks will deny it but
One reason why they go
Is to get the latest "Low Down"
On the people whom they know. —Albert E. May

♦ ♦ ♦

Don't follow fashion blindly into every dark alley. Always remember that you are not a model or mannequin for which the fashion is created. —Marlene Dietrich

W.C. Fields: "Women are like elephants. I like to look at them but I wouldn't want to own one. . . . I was in love with a beautiful blonde once. 'Twas a woman drove me to drink, and I never had the decency to write and thank her."

◆ ◆ ◆

You are not tempted because you are evil; you are tempted because you are human.   —Bishop Fulton J. Sheen

◆ ◆ ◆

Little Nancy, trying to be helpful on the farm, returned from the henhouse and went to her grandmother to report: "There aren't any eggs, Granny, but all the seats are taken."

◆ ◆ ◆

Middle age: when you are sitting at home on Saturday night and the telephone rings and you hope it isn't for you. —Ring Lardner

◆ ◆ ◆

No matter what other nations may say about us—immigration is still the sincerest form of flattery.

◆ ◆ ◆

If laser beams can cut through mountains, why should we doubt the power of prayer?   —William Arthur Ward

Little Boy Blue . . .

The little toy dog is covered with dust,
   But sturdy and staunch he stands;
And the little toy soldier is red with rust,
   And his musket molds in his hands;
Time was when the little toy dog was new,
   And the soldier was passing fair;
And that was the time when our Little Boy Blue
   Kissed them and put them there.

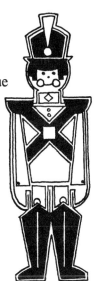

"Now, don't you go till I come," he said,
   "And don't you make any noise!"
So toddling off to his trundle-bed
   He dreamed of the pretty toys;
And, as he was dreaming, an angel song
   Awakened our Little Boy Blue—
Oh! the years are many, the years are long,
   But the little toy friends are true!

Ay, faithful to Little Boy Blue they stand,
   Each in the same old place
Awaiting the touch of a little hand,
   And the smile of a little face;
And they wonder, as waiting these long years through
   In the dust of that little chair,
What has become of our Little Boy Blue,
   Since he kissed them and put them there.   —Eugene Field

♦ ♦ ♦

If a friend of mine . . . gave a feast, and did not invite me to it, I should not mind a bit. . . . But if . . . a friend of mine had a sorrow and refused to allow me to share it, I should feel it most bitterly . . .   —Oscar Wilde

♦ ♦ ♦

Reading maketh a full man, conference a ready man, and writing an exact man.   —Francis Bacon

Our founding fathers did not hand any generation of Americans a neatly packaged, ready-made America. Instead they handed us a set of tools—principles and institutions—for us to use in shaping the kind of nation we want. The people must win and rewin America in every generation.   —George Romney

♦ ♦ ♦

A woman bought a new wig and thought it would be a good joke to surprise her husband at the office. She walked in on him and asked: "Do you think you could find a place in your life for a woman like me?"

"Not a chance," he snapped. "You remind me too much of my wife."

♦ ♦ ♦

You grow up the first time you laugh—at yourself.
                                                        —Ethel Barrymore

♦ ♦ ♦

The late Wilfrid Funk, who spent a lifetime exploring the English language, once compiled a list of what he considered the ten most beautiful words—dawn, hush, lullaby, murmuring, tranquil, mist, luminous, chimes, golden, and melody. Compare these to the ten most unpleasant words—belch, grub, slop, ground, asphalt, scratch, quack, backache, hunk, and crabgrass.

♦ ♦ ♦

Though I speak with the tongues of men and of angels, and have not charity, I am become as sounding brass, or a tinkling cymbal.
                                                        —I Corinthians 13:1

♦ ♦ ♦

The secret of contentment is knowing how to enjoy what you have, and to be able to lose all desire for things beyond your reach.
                                                        —Lin Yutang

76

His (Woodrow Wilson's) addresses were almost invariably extemporaneous, although he prepared his outlines with care. Once when he was asked by some undergraduates to make a speech he inquired how long it should be. "It doesn't matter," he was told. "It matters to me," he replied. "If you want me to talk for ten minutes, I need two weeks to prepare. If you want me to speak for half an hour I need a day. If you have no time limit I am ready right now."   —Raymond B. Fosdick

♦ ♦ ♦

The trouble with being pleasant is people think you're a hypocrite.   —Franklin P. Jones

♦ ♦ ♦

Law is the rampart that keeps barbarism from rolling across America like a deluge. It is the positive force of reason, custom and sanity which keeps our volatile, often overheated society from exploding.   —Editorial, *Indianapolis Star*

♦ ♦ ♦

And he would want some place to be
Where hate and greed he'd never see.
And so on lakes and streams and brooks
The Good Lord fashioned fishing nooks.

♦ ♦ ♦

Led by an old Indian, tourists were visiting the ruins of an Indian temple. To reach the ancient shrine they had to leave their cars at a distance. Suddenly one woman exclaimed: "Oh, I forgot to lock my car."

"Don't worry," said the Indian guide. "There isn't a white man within 50 miles of here."

The gobbledegook that finds its way into business communications is often annoying and sometimes funny. The following directive from the British Admiralty is a classic of the genre: "It is necessary for technical reasons that these warheads should be stored upside down, that is, with the top at the bottom and the bottom at the top. In order that there may be no doubt as to which is the bottom and which the top, for storage purposes, it will be seen that the bottom of each warhead has been labeled with the word 'Top.' "

♦ ♦ ♦

More wives are returning to work so they can afford to buy those new labor-saving devices, which give them the freedom to go to work.

♦ ♦ ♦

When Joe Louis was asked who had hit him the hardest during his ring career, he shrugged, "That's easy—Uncle Sam!"

♦ ♦ ♦

Is life so dear or peace so sweet, as to be purchased at the price of chains and slavery? Forbid it, Almighty God! —Patrick Henry

♦ ♦ ♦

Liberty lies in the hearts of men and women; when it dies there, no constitution, no law, no court can save it.
                                                    —Judge Learned Hand

♦ ♦ ♦

Our union is now complete; our constitution composed, established, and approved. You are now the guardians of your own liberties.   —Samuel Adams

After watching the squabbles that often develop in the splitting up of estates, we can sympathize with the old fellow whose will contained only the following: "Being of sound mind, I spent every cent I had."

♦ ♦ ♦

Happiness is a butterfly, which when pursued is always just beyond your grasp, but which, if you will sit down quietly, may alight upon you.
—Nathaniel Hawthorne

♦ ♦ ♦

There is only one terminal dignity—love. And the story of a love is not important—what is important is that one is capable of love. It is perhaps the only glimpse we are permitted of eternity.
—Helen Hayes

♦ ♦ ♦

The best cure for worry, depression, melancholy, and brooding is to go deliberately forth and try to lift with one's sympathy the gloom of somebody else.   —Arnold Bennett

♦ ♦ ♦

A Chinaman once remarked that he could write the biography of the average American in three chapters, using the following chapter headings: "Hurry," "Worry," and "Bury."

♦ ♦ ♦

They can say all they want about being over the hill. It still beats being under it.

Sea-Fever . . .

I must go down to the seas again,
   to the lonely sea and the sky,
And all I ask is a tall ship and a star to steer her by,
And the wheel's kick and the wind's song
   and the white sail's shaking,
And a grey mist on the sea's face and a
   grey dawn breaking.

I must go down to the seas again, for the
   call of the running tide
Is a wild call and a clear call that may not be denied;
And all I ask is a windy day with the
   white clouds flying,
And the flung spray and the blown spume
   and the sea-gulls crying.

I must go down to the seas again to the vagrant gypsy life,
To the gull's way and the whale's way where the wind's like
   a whetted knife;
And all I ask is a merry yarn from a laughing fellow-rover,
And quiet sleep and a sweet dream when the long trick's over.
—John Masefield

♦ ♦ ♦

The great enemy of the truth is very often not the lie—deliberate, contrived, and dishonest—but the myth—persistent, persuasive, and unrealistic.   —John F. Kennedy

♦ ♦ ♦

What is a weed? A plant whose virtues have not yet been discovered.   —Ralph Waldo Emerson

♦ ♦ ♦

People who don't have nightmares don't have dreams.
—Robert Paul Smith

A woman went to the office of the local paper and said she would like to put a notice in about her husband's disappearance. "How much will it cost?" she asked.

"We charge fifty cents an inch," the editor said.

"Oh, I can't afford that kind of money," said the woman, "My husband is six feet tall!"

♦ ♦ ♦

There was an old woman who lived in a shoe. She had so many children she ran out of names to call her husband. —Tom Roberts

♦ ♦ ♦

"Well, doctor, was my operation a success?"
"Who's a doctor? I'm St. Peter."

♦ ♦ ♦

. . . It is far more seemly to have thy studie full of books, than thy purse full of money.   —John Lyly

♦ ♦ ♦

The best test for morality is to ask yourself, "Is it good manners?" This might sound absurd, but it is a true criterion, Every immoral act contains an element of bad manners since it disregards the rights and feelings of others. Jonathan Swift said it best: "Good manners is the art of making people comfortable. Whoever makes the fewest persons uneasy is the best bred in the company." To this I would like to add—he is also the most moral.
                                                                —Ann Landers

♦ ♦ ♦

"Hasty love is soon hot and soon cold."   —Old Proverb

Perseverance is more prevailing than violence; and many things which cannot be overcome when they are together, yield themselves up when taken little by little.   —Plutarch

♦ ♦ ♦

Some persons not only expect opportunity to knock, but they want it to break the door down.

♦ ♦ ♦

Not many sounds in life, and I include all urban and all rural sounds, exceed in interest a knock at the door.   —Charles Lamb

♦ ♦ ♦

If you don't believe a ten-year-old boy can keep a secret, ask him where he left the family hammer.

♦ ♦ ♦

The youngster next door is not completely useless. At least five mothers use him for a bad example.

♦ ♦ ♦

The difference between machines and human beings is that human beings can be reproduced by unskilled labor.
                                                    —Arthur Clark

♦ ♦ ♦

Laws are always unstable unless they are founded on the manners of a nation; and manners are the only durable and resisting power in a people.   —Alexis de Tocqueville

In the early days of the Federal Government it was customary for the Representatives to wear their hats during the sessions of the House. When speaking the Representative uncovered and held his hat in his hand, placed it on the benches or gave it to another member to hold. . . . It was not until after the close of President Jackson's administration in 1837 that this practice was discontinued.

♦ ♦ ♦

Just about the time a woman thinks her work is done, she becomes a grandmother.

♦ ♦ ♦

Business is what, when you don't have any, you go out of.
—The Guardian

♦ ♦ ♦

Conceit is God's gift to little men.　　　　　—Bruce Barton

♦ ♦ ♦

Lord Chesterfield told his son, "Make the other person like himself a little bit more and I promise you that he will like you very much indeed."

♦ ♦ ♦

I like the dreams of the future better than the history of the past.
—Thomas Jefferson

♦ ♦ ♦

There is more to life than increasing its speed.
—Mahatma Gandhi

♦ ♦ ♦

No opportunity is ever lost—the other fellow takes those you've missed.

If God shuts one door, he opens another.   —Irish Proverb

♦ ♦ ♦

We always like those who admire us; we do not always like those whom we admire.   —François, Duc de La Rochefoucauld

♦ ♦ ♦

Today's timely question: How do you explain counter-clockwise to a youngster with a digital watch?

♦ ♦ ♦

"Every man has the love affairs he deserves."
                                        —Arthur Pendenys

♦ ♦ ♦

"Love is the delusion that one woman differs from another."
                                        —H.L. Mencken

♦ ♦ ♦

It seems to me that the book is the most important tool that man has ever invented, more important than wheels, cement, or running water. . . . For me the book is the recorded wisdom of man from the beginning of time; and the recorded evil as well. The book is the way we trace our heritage; enunciate our values; understand what we are as human beings. The book is the great flame, the lasting flame that never goes out and hopefully will never go out, that bears our despairs as well as our achievements. Everything that man has ever aspired to do or thought or felt is embraced within the cover of a book. The book is a magnificent art form. The book is man's immortality.   —Irving Stone

♦ ♦ ♦

The bitterness of poor quality remains long after the sweetness of low price is forgotten.

Native ladies of central Africa are dismayed by the topless swimsuit fad in America. They're afraid the *National Geographic* will stop sending photographers.   —Jack Wilson

♦ ♦ ♦

About three o'clock one morning the telephone rang in Dr. Gallup's house. Sleepily the king of public opinion polls got out of bed and lifted the receiver.

"Is this Dr. Gallup?" said the voice at the other end of the line.

"Yes, yes. What do you want?"

"I've just rung up to tell you I've changed my mind."

♦ ♦ ♦

If you want to speed a package through the mails try stamping it "Fresh Fish."   —Lane Olinghouse

Anyone can buy new things, but only a strong man can throw out old things.

♦ ♦ ♦

He has half the deed done, who has made a beginning.
                    —Horace

♦ ♦ ♦

How majestic is naturalness. I have never met a man whom I really considered a great man who was not always natural and simple. Affectation is inevitably the mark of one not sure of himself.   —Charles G. Dawes

♦ ♦ ♦

It is disgraceful to stumble against the same stone twice.
                    —Greek Proverb

♦ ♦ ♦

A good scare is more effective than good advice.

What most people are looking for these days is less to do, more time to do it in, and more pay for not getting it done.

♦ ♦ ♦

If thou wouldst conquer thy weakness thou must not gratify it.
—William Penn

♦ ♦ ♦

The test of good manners is to be able to put up pleasantly with bad ones.
—Wendell Willkie

♦ ♦ ♦

Humor has a hundred faces; tragedy only a few.
—H.G. Mendelson

♦ ♦ ♦

Melancholy sees the worst of things—things as they might be, and not as they are.
—Christian Bovee

♦ ♦ ♦

Romance is like a game of chess—one false move and you're mated.

♦ ♦ ♦

When I was growing up, four of us kids slept in one bed. It was pretty crowded when we got older, so my mother made me a bed of my own by putting a board between two chairs. I always dreamed of the day when I'd be able to afford a mattress. Finally I got there. I bought myself the biggest, softest mattress I could find. But then I got terrible backaches. I went to a doctor and asked what I could do for my sore back. He said, "Sleep on a board!"

—Sam Levenson

When George Washington took the oath as first President of the United States on April 30, 1789, he spontaneously added this four-word prayer of his own: "So help me God," an invocation still used in official oaths by those taking public office, in courts of justice, and in other legal proceedings.

♦ ♦ ♦

Always remember—golf is like a beautiful woman. You can't take either for granted.
—Dan Valentine

♦ ♦ ♦

Grandma may have worked harder as a housewife, but she never had to clean out the swimming pool, mix a Martini, or get the power mower started.

♦ ♦ ♦

To entertain some people all you have to do is sit and listen.

♦ ♦ ♦

Women's rear ends just weren't made for pants. —Coco Chanel

♦ ♦ ♦

Love is the only fire against which there is no insurance.
—Edith Piaf

♦ ♦ ♦

A small town telephone operator received a call each day for the correct time. One day she asked the caller why he phoned each day for the time.

"I have to know the exact time," he explained, "so I can blow the town whistle right at noon." "My goodness," the operator gasped. "I always set my clock by your whistle."

When the new preacher loaned his fine team of horses to a friend he cautioned: instead of "giddy-up!" to start them you say "Praise the Lord!"; and in place of "Whoa!", shout "Amen!"

The fellow broke over the crown of a hill and started down at full gallop, when he noticed that the bridge was out at the bottom. "Whoa!" he screamed repeatedly as they approached the danger point; then, just before they plunged over he remembered, and yelled, "Amen!" They stopped.

He sighed, mopped his brow and breathed, "Praise the Lord!"

♦ ♦ ♦

Creativeness often consists of merely turning up what is already there. Did you know that right and left shoes were thought up only a little more than a century ago?   —Bernice Fitzgibbon

♦ ♦ ♦

Subtlety is the art of saying what you think and getting out of range before it is understood.

♦ ♦ ♦

A little girl was telling her mother about her day's activities. "We played 'Wedding,' " she said. "I was the bride, Elsie was the bridesmaid, and Elsie's little sister the flower girl."

"Who was the groom?" the mother asked.

"Oh, I wanted a small wedding," the child replied, "so we didn't have a groom."

♦ ♦ ♦

We are told that the weaker sex is really the stronger sex. This is due solely to the weakness of the "stronger sex" for the weaker sex.

In Flanders Fields .   .

In Flanders fields the poppies blow
Between the crosses, row on row.
   That mark our place; and in the sky
   The larks, still bravely singing, fly
Scarce heard amid the guns below.

We are the Dead. Short days ago
We lived, felt dawn, saw sunset glow,
   Loved and were loved, and now we lie
      In Flanders fields.

Take up our quarrel with the foe;
To you from failing hands we throw
   The torch; be yours to hold it high.
   If ye break faith with us who die
We shall not sleep, though poppies grow
      In Flanders fields.   —John McCrea

◆ ◆ ◆

The door-to-door salesman rang the bell in a suburban home
and the door opened, revealing a nine-year-old boy who was
puffing on a long, black cigar. Trying to cover his amazement, the
salesman said: "Good morning, sonny. Is your mother in?"
   The boy removed the cigar from his mouth, flicked off its ashes,
and replied: "What do *you* think?"

◆ ◆ ◆

Every year I live I am more convinced that the waste of life lies
in the love we have not given; the powers we had not used; the
selfish prudence which will risk nothing and which, shrinking
pain, misses happiness as well.   —John B. Tabb

◆ ◆ ◆

The man who has a full set of tools has no children.

The nomination of Lincoln in 1860 cost his friends less than $700. Judge David Davis, one of Lincoln's intimates, told Sen. John J. Ingalls of Kansas that this covered everything "including headquarters, telegraphing, music, fare of delegates, incidentals." That, of course, was some time ago.

♦ ♦ ♦

It is related that a business friend once wrote to Mark Twain, asking his opinion on a matter of mutual interest. He waited several days, then wrote again. The second letter was ignored. Then a third letter was sent, enclosing a sheet of paper and a two-cent stamp. That spurred the overworked humorist to action. By return mail Mark sent a postal card, on which was crudely typed:

"Paper and stamp received. Please send envelope."

♦ ♦ ♦

Women will never be as successful as men because they have no wives to advise them.　　　　　　　　　—Dick Van Dyke

♦ ♦ ♦

Young Jerry had just introduced his very blonde and glamorous girlfriend to his family.

"What do you think, Mom?" he whispered proudly. "Some dish, huh?"

"That she is!" the mother agreed, "but is she kitchen-tested?"

♦ ♦ ♦

A man has to live with himself; he should see that he always has good company.

♦ ♦ ♦

The surest way to catch a waiter's eye is by owning the restaurant.

Can you name the author of these familiar quotes? (answers below)

1. Man is his own worst enemy.
2. Let us do or die.
3. Candy
   Is dandy
   But liquor
   Is quicker.
4. Absence makes the heart grow fonder.
5. His bark is worse than his bite.
6. Into each life some rain must fall,
   Some days must be dark and dreary.
7. Nothing is certain but death and taxes.
8. Oh, what a tangled web we weave,
   When first we practice to deceive!
9. Handsome is that handsome does.
10. We have met the enemy, and they are ours.

1. Cicero
2. Robert Burns, *Bannockburn*
3. Ogden Nash, *Hard Lines* (1931).
4. T.H. Bayly, *Isle of Beauty*
5. George Herbert, *Jacula Prudentum*
6. Henry Wadsworth Longfellow, *The Rainy Day*
7. Benjamin Franklin, *Letter to M. Leroy*
8. Sir Walter Scott, *Marmion*
9. Oliver Goldsmith, *The Vicar of Wakefield*
10. Oliver H. Perry, *Dispatch to General Harrison*

◆ ◆ ◆

For anyone to achieve something, he will have to show a little courage. You're only on this earth once. You must give out all you've got. —Ethel Kennedy

◆ ◆ ◆

By all means use sometimes to be alone. Salute thyself; see what thy soul doth wear. —George Herbert

◆ ◆ ◆

Good judgment comes from experience, and experience comes from poor judgment.

Choose an author as you choose a friend.
                    —Wentworth Dillon, Lord of Roscommon

♦ ♦ ♦

Today . . .

There are two days in every week about which we should not
worry, two days which should be kept from fear and apprehension.

One of these days is Yesterday with its mistakes and cares, its
faults and blunders, its aches and pains. Yesterday has passed
forever beyond our control.

All the money in the world cannot bring back yesterday. We
cannot erase a single word we said. Yesterday is gone.

The other day we should not worry about is Tomorrow with its
possible adversities, its burdens, its large promise, and poor
performance. Tomorrow is also beyond our immediate control.

Tomorrow's sun will rise, either in splendor or behind a mask of
clouds—but it will rise. Until it does, we have no stake in Tomorrow, for it is yet unborn.

This leaves only one day—Today. Any man can fight the battles
of just one day. It is only when you and I add the burdens of those
two awful eternities—Yesterday and Tomorrow—that we break
down.

It is not the experience of Today that drives men mad—it is
remorse or bitterness for something which happened Yesterday
and the dread of what will happen Tomorrow.

♦ ♦ ♦

Dr. Charles W. Eliot, the eminent educator of Harvard whose
fate it has been to be dubiously immortalized by a five-foot shelf
of books, was once asked how Harvard had gained its prestige as
the greatest storehouse of knowledge in the nation.

"In all likelihood," said Dr. Eliot slyly, "it is because the
freshman bring so much of it, and the seniors take away so little."

♦ ♦ ♦

What do the phrases, "clean as a hound's tooth," "the lunatic
fringe," "pussyfooting," "Molly-coddle," and "rubber stamp
congress" have in common? They were all coined by Teddy
Roosevelt.

Some airlines would like to eliminate cocktails, gourmet meals, in-flight movies, and all the other extras they now provide—but they're afraid that without those frills passengers would suddenly realize they're six miles up.

♦ ♦ ♦

A man went into a lumberyard and said he wanted a 2 × 4. The salesman asked him "How long do you want it?"

The man said, "Just a minute, I'll go ask my friend."

He came back and said, "My friend says we want it for a long time."

♦ ♦ ♦

In the final analysis, it's true that fame is unimportant. No matter how great a man is, the size of his funeral usually depends on the weather. —Rosemary Clooney

♦ ♦ ♦

Tact is changing the subject without changing your mind.

♦ ♦ ♦

The man that blushes is not quite a brute. —Edward Young

♦ ♦ ♦

"You've been acquitted of the charge of bigamy," the judge told the defendant. "You're free to go home to your wife."

"Which one?" asked the man.

Epitaphs . . .

On a grave in Burlington, Vermont: "She lived with her husband fifty years and died in the confident hope of a better life."

"Here I lie snug as a bug in a rug."
An envious relative directed that he be laid to rest in an adjoining grave with the following inscription over him: "Here I lie snugger than that other bugger."

Over the grave of a man in Ohio: "Too bad for Heaven, too good for Hell, so, where he's gone, I cannot tell."

A gravestone in a church cemetery in Buferd, England: "In this place lies William Yeast. Pardon him for not rising."

In Buferd, England, over the grave of Sir John Strange: "Here lies an honest lawyer—and that is strange!"

On a New England tombstone: "I told you I was sick, Elizabeth."

♦ ♦ ♦

It seems the neighbor's boy just can't win. He was kicked out of parochial school for swearing and out of public school for praying.

♦ ♦ ♦

A chip on the shoulder is a sure indication that there is more wood higher up.   —Aldous Huxley

♦ ♦ ♦

Most of us can run pretty well all day on one good compliment.

♦ ♦ ♦

A news story tells about a woman whose husband gave her 25 cents a day for spending money and she saved all these quarters until she had enough to buy a divorce. Seems like it just doesn't pay a man to be nice to some women.

Not long ago the psychology department of a great university conducted an investigation to discover just why certain persons were disliked by their associates and acquaintances. Many causes of unpopularity were uncovered, but the one that ranked at the top was the failure to keep promises.

Don't pledge yourself to do something unless you are reasonably sure that you will be able to make good. But once you have given your word, then go to any length to keep it. That's the way to avoid being the most disliked of all persons, one who fails to keep his promises.

◆ ◆ ◆

Letter from collection manager to delinquent customer:

"Dear Sir: If you don't pay me what you owe me, I'll tell your creditors that you did."

◆ ◆ ◆

Chance is perhaps the pseudonym of God when He did not want to sign.　　　　　　　　　　　　　　　　—Anatole France

◆ ◆ ◆

They had just had a lover's spat, and as the youth was leaving his girlfriend's house he encountered her kid brother. "Your sister's a little spoiled, isn't she?" he commented.

"No," was the kid brother's reply. "That's just the perfume she's wearing."

◆ ◆ ◆

Victor Borge boasted to a friend that he could tell the time by the piano. To prove his point he sat down and crashed into a few bars of a Sousa march. Immediately there was a pounding on the hotel wall and a sleepy voice rumbled angrily: "Stop that noise, you idiot. It's 1:30 in the morning."

More Gravestone Epitaphs . .

Epitaph in Enosburg Falls, Vt.:
"In memory of
Anna Hopewell
Here lies the body of our Anna
Done to death by a banana
It wasn't the fruit that laid her low
But the skin of the thing that made her go "

A simple epitaph on a simple man in Tennessee:
"He was a simple man who died of complications."

On a hanged sheep-stealer from Bletchley, Bucks, England:
"Here lies the body of Thomas Kemp
Who lived by wool and died by hemp"

On William Wilson in Lambeth, London, England:
"Here Lieth W. W.
Who never more will
Trouble you, trouble you."

Epitaph in Chattanooga, Tennessee:
"I came into this world
Without my consent
And left in the same manner."

♦ ♦ ♦

There is no worse robber than a bad book.   —Italian Proverb

♦ ♦ ♦

Teacher—"Now, Tommy, tell me where elephants are found."
Tommy—"Elephants are such very large animals they hardly
ever get lost."

♦ ♦ ♦

Good breeding consists in concealing how much we think of
ourselves and how little we think of the other person.
—Mark Twain

♦ ♦ ♦

No man iz ritch who wants enny more than what he haz got.
—Josh Billings

Education is an ornament in prosperity and a refuge in adversity.   —Aristotle

♦ ♦ ♦

Fine art is that in which the hand, the head, and the heart go together.   —John Ruskin

♦ ♦ ♦

There is little that can withstand a man who can conquer himself.   —Louis XIV

♦ ♦ ♦

If you don't think women are explosive, try dropping one.

♦ ♦ ♦

Work keeps us from three great evils: boredom, vice, and need.
                                                         —Voltaire

♦ ♦ ♦

Pleasure is labor too, and tires as much.   —William Cowper

♦ ♦ ♦

Nothing deteriorates your car so fast as your neighbor buying a new one.

♦ ♦ ♦

Is not a life a hundred times too short for us to bore ourselves?
                                     —Friedrich Wilhelm Nietzsche

♦ ♦ ♦

Wouldn't it be nice to hear just one joke about the saleswoman and the farmer's son?

CROSSING KANSAS BY TRAIN

The telephone poles
have been holding their
arms out
a long time now
to birds
that will not
settle there
but pass with
strange cawings
westward to
where dark trees
gather about
a waterhole. This
is Kansas. The
mountains start here
just behind
the closed eyes
of farmers'
sons asleep
in their workclothes.

—Donald Justice

♦ ♦ ♦

The masterpiece, Mona Lisa, was actually rejected by the subject's husband, Francesco del Giocondo of Florence, because he didn't like it. The king of France, Francis I, bought the painting for his bathroom in 1517. During 1962 the infamous painting was moved from Washington, D.C. to New York City, and was assessed for insurance purposes at $100 million.

♦ ♦ ♦

An elderly woman was waiting for a parking space in a Palm Beach shopping center. The occupant pulled out and from seemingly nowhere a young kid zipped into the empty space with his Corvette. The lady said, "You saw me waiting for that space!"

The young man chuckled and said, "Well, that's what you can do when you're young and fast."

He started to walk away and the woman began to dent his sports car with her cane. "What are you doing?" he screamed. The lady replied, "This is what you can do when you're old and rich!"

98

Take Heart!

During its first year the Coca Cola Company sold only 400 cokes.

Dr. Seuss's first children's book was rejected by 23 publishers. The 24th publisher sold 6 million copies.

During his first three years in the automobile business Henry Ford went bankrupt twice.

After being rejected by both Hewlett-Packard and Atari, Apple micro-computer had first year sales of $2.5 million.

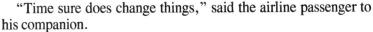

"Time sure does change things," said the airline passenger to his companion.

"When I was a boy, I used to sit in a flat-bottomed boat on that lake down there below and fish. Every time a plane flew over I'd look up and wish I were in it. Now I look down and wish I were fishing."

♦ ♦ ♦

Woman to marriage counselor: "The only thing my husband and I have in common is that we were married the same day."

♦ ♦ ♦

5 WAYS TO BREAK AN ENGAGEMENT . . .

1. Ask if she'd mind changing clothes with you.
2. Shower her with gifts of different mouthwash.
3. Tell her you always take out large insurance policies on all your wives.
4. At a really passionate moment, call her "Mommy."
5. Say that your mother, an interior decorator, must live with you.

Meeting at Night . . .

I.

The gray sea and the long black land;
And the yellow half-moon large and low.
And the startled little waves that leap
In fiery ringlets from their sleep,
As I gain the cove with pushing prow,
And quench its speed i' the slushy sand.

II.

Then a mile of warm, sea-scented beach.
Three fields to cross till a farm appears;
A tap at the pane, the quick sharp scratch
And blue spurt of a lighted match,
And a voice less loud, thro' its joys and
    fears,
Then the two hearts beating each to each!   —Robert Browning

◆ ◆ ◆

Sam Goldwyn, the movie producer, used to mangle the English language so badly that his malaprops and mixed metaphors came to be known as Goldwynisms. Some that have become classics are:
    "A verbal contract isn't worth the paper it's printed on."
    "Every Tom, Dick, and Harry is named William."
    "Now, gentlemen, listen slowly."
    "For your information, I would like to ask a question."
    "Don't talk to me while I'm interrupting."
    "I may not always be right, but I'm never wrong."

◆ ◆ ◆

We went to the King's theater, where we saw *A Midsummer Night's Dream,* which I had never seen before, nor shall ever again, for it is the most insipid, ridiculous play that I ever saw in my life.   —Samuel Pepys

100

"What does a billion dollars mean to you, who is all-powerful?" a man asked God.

"Hardly a penny," God replied.

"And what are a hundred thousand centuries?"

"Hardly a second."

"Then, O Lord, give me a penny," the man begged.

"In a second."

♦ ♦ ♦

Preparing to discuss electricity, the professor asked the class if anyone knew just what electricity was. A student in the back put his arm up hesitantly for a moment or two and then plucked it back down. The old professor saw this but asked him again anyway: "What is electricity?"

"I forget," came the sheepish reply.

"Ach," the professor exploded. "The only man in the world who knows what electricity is, and he forgets!"

♦ ♦ ♦

Ideals are like stars; you will not succeed in touching them with your hands. But like the seafaring man on the desert of waters, you choose them as your guides, and following them you will reach your destiny.   —Carl Schurz

♦ ♦ ♦

A little boy needing a minor operation was taken to the hospital. His ward had an intercom system by which the floor nurse could talk to her patients. That night, however, her efforts to reach the boy were in vain. "Timmy," she said into the intercom, "I know you're there. Why don't you answer me?"

There was a long pause. Then a small, quavering voice asked, "What do you want, Wall?"

101

DEATH SPEAKS: There was a merchant in Bagdad who sent his servant to market to buy provisions and in a little while the servant came back, white and trembling, and said, "Master, just now when I was in the market-place I was jostled by a woman in the crowd and when I turned I saw it was Death that jostled me. She looked at me and made a threatening gesture; now, lend me your horse, and I will ride away from this city and avoid my fate. I will go to Samarra and there Death will not find me."

The merchant lent him his horse, and the servant mounted it, and he dug his spurs in its flank and as fast as the horse could gallop he went. Then the merchant went down to the market-place and he saw me standing in the crowd and he came to me and said, "Why did you make a threatening gesture to my servant when you saw him this morning?" "That was not a threatening gesture," I said, "it was only a start of surprise. I was astonished to see him in Bagdad, for I had an appointment with him tonight in Samarra."

—W. Somerset Maugham

♦ ♦ ♦

Dr. Karl Menninger was asked at a forum once what a person should do if he felt a nervous breakdown coming on. The famous psychiatrist said, ". . . lock up your house, go across the railroad tracks, and find someone in need and do something for him."

♦ ♦ ♦

Cleaning out the kids' room while they're still at home is like shoveling your sidewalk while it's still snowing.

♦ ♦ ♦

What loneliness is more lonely than distrust?   —George Eliot

102

The story is told that Winston Churchill hailed a cab in the West End and told the cabbie to drive him to BBC, where he was scheduled to make a speech to the world.

"Sorry, sir," said the driver. "Ye'll have to get yourself another cab. I can't go that far."

Mr. Churchill was somewhat surprised, and asked the cabbie why his field of operations was so limited.

"It hain't ordinarily, sir," apologized the driver, "but ye see, sir, Mr. Churchill is broadcasting in an hour, and I wants to get 'ome to 'ear 'im."

Mr. Churchill was so well pleased that he pulled out a pound note and handed it to the driver, who took one quick look at it and said: "Hop in, sir. The devil with Mr. Churchill."

♦ ♦ ♦

Gov. Jerry Apodaca visited the elementary school in East Grand Plains, New Mexico, and offered to answer questions from the children.

One first-grade boy put up his hand and asked, "Can we go outside and play?"

♦ ♦ ♦

Sign in a small filling station located too many miles from anywhere: "Don't ask us for information. If we knew anything we wouldn't be here."

♦ ♦ ♦

"Mummy, may I go in for a swim?" the child asked his mother. "Certainly not, my dear; it's far too deep," the mother responded. "But Daddy is swimming," the son said, "Yes," the mother answered, "but he's insured."

News item in an 1868 New York paper: "A man has been arrested in New York for attempting to extort funds from ignorant and superstitious people by exhibiting a device which he says will convey the human voice any distance over metallic wires so that it will be heard by the listener at the other end. He calls the instrument a telephone. Well-informed people know that it is impossible to transmit the human voice over wires."

♦ ♦ ♦

I must say I like bright colors. When I get to heaven I mean to spend a considerable portion of my first million years in painting. I expect orange and vermillion will be the dullest colors upon my palette, and beyond them will be a whole range of wonderful new colors which will delight the celestial eye.   —Winston Churchill

♦ ♦ ♦

Not in the clamor of the crowded street,
Not in the shouts and plaudits of the throng,
But in ourselves, are triumph and defeat.
                        —Henry Wadsworth Longfellow

♦ ♦ ♦

Many people take no care of their money till they come nearly to the end of it, and others do just the same with their time.
                        —Johann Wolfgang von Goethe

♦ ♦ ♦

A man who hoards up riches and enjoys them not is like an ass that carries gold and eats thistles.   —Sir Richard Francis Burton

SOME ODDITIES

Here are some geographical oddities compiled by the National Geography society:

The city of Reno, Nevada, is 100 miles further west than Los Angeles.

Jacksonville, Florida, is further west than Cleveland, Ohio.

One travels south from Detroit to reach the nearest part of Canada.

At Panama the sun rises in the Pacific and sets in the Atlantic—due to a gigantic bend in the isthmus.

The city of New York lies west of the Pacific—at least that part of the Pacific that touches western Chile.

♦ ♦ ♦

The way to live longer is to cut out all the things that make you want to live longer.

♦ ♦ ♦

Drive as you wish your kids would.

♦ ♦ ♦

Blessed are they who have nothing to say and cannot be persuaded to say it.

♦ ♦ ♦

A grade school teacher was instructing her youngsters on the value of coins. She took a half-dollar and laid it on her desk. "Can any of you tell me what it is?" she asked.

From the rear of the room came the shrill voice of a small boy: "Tails!"

Getting it Coming and Going . .

One hour after beginning a new job which involved moving a pile of bricks from the top of a two-story house to the ground, a construction worker in Peterborough, Ontario, suffered an accident which hospitalized him. He was instructed by his employer to fill out an accident report. It read:

"Thinking I could save time, I rigged a beam with a pulley at the top of the house, and a rope leading to the ground. I tied an empty barrel on one end of the rope, pulled it to the top of the house, and then fastened the other end of the rope to a tree. Going up to the top of the house, I filled the barrel with bricks.

"Then I went down and unfastened the rope to let the barrel down. Unfortunately the barrel of bricks was now heavier than I, and before I knew what was happening, the barrel jerked me up in the air. I hung on to the rope, and halfway up I met the barrel coming down, receiving a severe blow on the left shoulder. I then continued on to the top, banging my head on the beam and jamming my fingers in the pulley.

"When the barrel hit the ground, the bottom burst, spilling the bricks. As I was now heavier than the barrel, I started down at high speed. Halfway down, I met the empty barrel coming up, receiving several cuts and contusions from the sharp edges of the bricks.

"At this point, I must have become confused, because I let go of the rope. The barrel came down, striking me on the head, and I woke up in the hospital.

"I respectfully request sick leave."

♦ ♦ ♦

W. Somerset Maugham (reported by his secretary) on his ninety-first birthday: "Oh, hell, another birthday."

106

Practice does not make perfect; perfect practice makes pe
—Vince Lon

♦ ♦ ♦

Every child comes with the message that God is not yet discouraged of man.
—Rabindranath Tagore

♦ ♦ ♦

The deep-sea diver had scarcely gotten down to the bottom when a message came from the surface which left him in a dilemma.

"Come up quick," he was told. "The ship is sinking!"

♦ ♦ ♦

More men are killed by overwork than the importance of the world justifies.
—Rudyard Kipling

♦ ♦ ♦

At every party there are two kinds of people—those who want to go home and those who don't. The trouble is they are married to each other.
—E.A. Wiggam

♦ ♦ ♦

Next to being shot at and missed, nothing is quite as satisfying as an income tax refund.

♦ ♦ ♦

The first thing a child learns when he gets a drum is that he's never going to get another one.

♦ ♦ ♦

Talk is cheap—until you hire a lawyer.

When people start waiting in line to get out of this country instead of standing in line to get in, we can start worrying about our system.

♦ ♦ ♦

The best way of answering a bad argument is to let it go on.
—Sydney Smith

♦ ♦ ♦

Friendship is the only thing in the world concerning the usefulness of which all mankind are agreed.

♦ ♦ ♦

A woman is a creature who needs new shoes to go with the dress she has in mind to go with her old shoes.   —Dan Bennett

♦ ♦ ♦

I envy the beasts two things—their ignorance of evil to come, and their ignorance of what is said about them.   —Voltaire

♦ ♦ ♦

Retiring is such a dull step. If you're planning to retire you ought to shut up about it.   —Katharine Hepburn

♦ ♦ ♦

All men have their different objects of ambition—horses, dogs, money, honor, as the case may be, but for my own part I would rather have a good friend than all these put together.   —Socrates

♦ ♦ ♦

A clock's perfection is not its pace but its regularity.
—Marquis de Vauvenargues

He jests at scars that never felt a wound.
But soft! What light through yonder window breaks?
It is the east, and Juliet is the sun!   —William Shakespeare

♦ ♦ ♦

A man had just finished a meal in an Italian restaurant. On his way out he told the manager that the veal parmigiana was better than he had had on a recent trip to Italy.

"Of course," said the man, "over there they use domestic cheese. Here we use imported!"

♦ ♦ ♦

It is no sin to sell dear; but a sin to give ill measure.
—James Kelley

♦ ♦ ♦

Refrain from covetousness and thy estate shall prosper. —Plato

♦ ♦ ♦

Few things are needful to make the wise man happy, but nothing satisfies the fool; and this is the reason why so many of mankind are miserable.   —François, Duc de La Rochefoucauld

♦ ♦ ♦

If you want to succeed you must be prepared to fail.
—Garson Kanin

♦ ♦ ♦

The teacher had asked her small pupils to tell about their acts of kindness to dumb animals. After several heart-stirring stories, the teacher asked Tommy if he had anything to add. "Well," he replied rather proudly, "I kicked a boy once for kicking his dog."

It is a common mistake to suppose that Julius Caesar was the first Emperor of the Roman Empire. His highest office was that of dictator of the Republic, an office to which he was chosen four times—for eleven days in 49 B.C., for an indefinite period in 48, for ten years in 46, and for life in 44. The dictatorship was an emergency device never resorted to under the Republic except in serious crises and it was never intended to be more than a makeshift.

♦ ♦ ♦

A little four-year-old girl and a little three-year-old boy walked hand-in-hand up to the front door of a neighbor's house. Standing on her tiptoes, the little girl was just able to reach the doorbell. The lady of the house asked the little girl what it was she wanted, and the little girl said, "We're playing house. This is my husband and I am his wife. May we come in?"

Thoroughly enchanted by the scene confronting her, the lady said, "By all means, do come in." Once inside, she offered the children lemonade and cookies which they graciously accepted. When a second tall glass of lemonade was offered, the little girl refused by saying: "No thank you. We have to go now. My husband wet his pants."

♦ ♦ ♦

The man who is most slow in promising is most sure to keep his word.   —Jean Jacques Rousseau

♦ ♦ ♦

An atheist is a man who has no invisible means of support.
                                   —John Buchan, Lord Tweedsmuir

♦ ♦ ♦

When befriended, remember it;
When you befriend—forget it.   —Benjamin Franklin

110

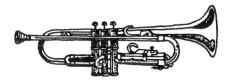

It is forbidden to kill, therefore all murderers are punished unless they kill in large numbers and to the sound of trumpets.

—Voltaire

♦ ♦ ♦

Here is a list of things for you to think on when you get the blues. They are but creature comforts, to be sure, but creature comforts have a certain pagan, non-moral power to soothe the soul, a peculiar power which neither religion nor philosophy possesses:

A chimney that draws well.

Real cream.

Sweet, perfect butter.

A fat book, containing a bully story, that will last a week.

A good bed waiting for you with open arms when you are sleepy and tired.

A spring of pure water.

A wood, in summer, with long grass, and a brook.

A new friend, who has never heard any of your jokes.

A woman whose face lights up when she sees you.

A man (if you're a woman) who likes you and is afraid of you.

Shoes that don't hurt.

The power to enjoy all these things and not be ashamed of yourself. —Dr. Frank Crane

♦ ♦ ♦

A forgiveness ought to be like a cancelled note, torn in two and burned up, so that it never can be shown against the man.

—Henry Ward Beecher

111

If you wish to be happy for an hour, get intoxicated. If you wish to be happy for three days, get married. If you wish to be happy for eight days, kill your pig and eat it. But if you wish to be happy forever, become a gardener. —Chinese Proverb

◆ ◆ ◆

Five-thousand-foot Mt. Maialeale, in Hawaii, averages 460 inches of rain a year. The driest place on earth is probably the Atacama desert, in Chile, where no measurable rainfall has been recorded for many years.

◆ ◆ ◆

The young man who has not wept is a savage, and the old man who will not laugh is a fool. —George Santayana

◆ ◆ ◆

The difference between estimated miles per gallon and what you actually get is about like the difference between salary and take home pay. —Doug Larson

◆ ◆ ◆

To receive a present handsomely and in a right spirit, even when you have none to give in return, is to give one in return.
—Leigh Hunt

◆ ◆ ◆

We should give as we would receive, cheerfully, quickly, and without hesitation; for there is no grace in a benefit that sticks to the fingers. —Seneca

◆ ◆ ◆

No man would listen to you talk if he didn't know it was his turn next. —Edgar Watson Howe

Unless you're ashamed of yourself now and then, you're not honest.   —William Feather

♦ ♦ ♦

A change of fortune hurts a wise man no more than a change of the moon.   —Benjamin Franklin

♦ ♦ ♦

Chance does nothing that has not been prepared beforehand.
                                            —Alexis de Tocqueville

♦ ♦ ♦

No man does anything from a single motive.
                                        —Samuel Taylor Coleridge

♦ ♦ ♦

The most difficult secret for a man to keep is his own opinion of himself.   —Marcel Pagnol

♦ ♦ ♦

Every many has a right to be conceited until he is successful.
                                                            —Disraeli

♦ ♦ ♦

The virtue lies in the struggle, not in the prize.
                                                  —Richard Milnes

♦ ♦ ♦

Give me my golf clubs, the fresh air and a beautiful partner, and you can keep my golf clubs and the fresh air.   —Jack Benny

♦ ♦ ♦

His thoughts were slow, his words were few and never formed to glisten, but he was joy to all his friends—you should have heard him listen.

(Part of Daniel Webster's speech in Congress in 1844 against an appropriation of $50,000 to establish mail communication with the Pacific Coast.)

"What do we want of the vast worthless area, this region of savages and wild beasts, of deserts of shifting sands and whirlwinds of dust, cactus, and prairie dogs? To what use could we ever hope to put these deserts, or these endless mountain ranges, impenetrable and covered to their bases with eternal snow? What can we ever hope to do with the western coast of three thousand miles, rockbound, cheerless and uninviting, with not a harbor in it. What use have we for such a country? Mr. President, I will never vote one cent from the public treasury to place the Pacific Coast one inch nearer Boston than it is today."

◆ ◆ ◆

This world presents enough problems if you believe it to be a world of law and order; do not add to them by believing it to be a world of miracles.　　　　　　—Justice Louis D. Brandeis

◆ ◆ ◆

Truly, our greatest blessings are very cheap.
　　　　　　　　　　　　　—Henry David Thoreau

◆ ◆ ◆

If I am building a mountain and stop before the last basketful of earth is placed on the summit I have failed.　　　—Confucius

◆ ◆ ◆

There's music in the sighing of a reed;
There's music in the gushing of a rill;
There's music in all things if men had ears;
There earth is but an echo of the spheres.　　　—Lord Byron

And this, too, shall pass away.   —Abraham Lincoln

◆ ◆ ◆

It is nothing to die; it is frightful not to live.   —Victor Hugo

◆ ◆ ◆

Let us have faith that right makes might, and in that faith let us to the end dare to do our duty as we understand it.

—Abraham Lincoln

◆ ◆ ◆

A meeting was being held at the churchhouse in a small, rural community to consider the purchase of a chandelier. Midway through the proceedings, an old fellow in the back row stood up and announced himself "agin" it.

"In the first place," he said, "we can't none of us spell it.

"In the second place, we can't none of us play it.

"And in the third place, we need some new light fixtures a lot worse than we need a chandelier!"

◆ ◆ ◆

Badges are for men not great enough in themselves.

◆ ◆ ◆

A man cannot think chiefly of himself without being discouraged.

◆ ◆ ◆

A decent provision for the poor is the true test of civilization.

—Samuel Johnson

◆ ◆ ◆

If education did nothing more than to open the great and vital books, giving us the ability to read ourselves into and out of them, its worth were beyond all price.   —John Lancaster Spalding

115

Song To Celia . . .

Drink to me only with thine eyes,
  And I will pledge with mine;
Or leave a kiss but in the cup,
  And I'll not look for wine.
The thirst that from the soul doth rise
  Doth ask a drink divine;
But might I of Jove's nectar sup,
  I would not change for thine.
I sent thee late a rosy wreath,
  Not so much honouring thee
As giving it a hope that there
  It could not withered be.
But thou thereon didst only breathe,
  And sent'st it back to me;
Since when it grows, and smells, I swear,
  Not of itself, but thee!
                                    —Ben Jonson

♦ ♦ ♦

Do not be in a hurry to succeed. What would you have to live for afterwards? Better make the horizon your goal; it will always be ahead of you.   —William Makepeace Thackeray

♦ ♦ ♦

Courage is not the absence of fear—it is the mastery of it.

♦ ♦ ♦

A college student wrote to his father: "Dear Father, I am broke, and have no friends. What shall I do?"
His Father's answer: "Make friends at once."

♦ ♦ ♦

In this world there are only two tragedies. One is not getting what one wants, and the other is getting it. The last is much the worst.   —Oscar Wilde

116

Some books are to be tasted, others to be swallowed, and some few to be chewed and digested.   —Francis Bacon

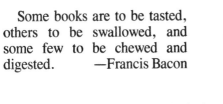

♦ ♦ ♦

We'd hate to have to shuffle off before we see how civilization wriggles out of this one.   —*Cottage Grove Sentinel* (Ore.)

♦ ♦ ♦

What is the most important ingredient in the making of a President? Luck. You must be where the lightning strikes. The decisive factor is how you maneuver yourself to attract the attention of the kingmakers, the power brokers, the press, and ultimately the people.   —Theodore H. White

♦ ♦ ♦

Every time I fill a vacant office I make ten malcontents and one ingrate.   —Louis XIV

♦ ♦ ♦

Modesty in delivering our opinions leaves us the liberty of changing them without humiliation.

♦ ♦ ♦

God be thanked for books. They are the voices of the distant and the dead, and make us heirs of the spiritual life of past ages.
                —William E. Channing

117

As a beauty I'm not a great star,
There are others more handsome by far,
    But my face I don't mind it,
    Because I'm behind it—
'Tis the folks in the front that I jar.

◆ ◆ ◆

When you flee from temptation—be sure you don't leave a forwarding address.

◆ ◆ ◆

We measure success by accumulation. The measure is false. The true measure is appreciation. He who loves most has most.
    —Henry Van Dyke

◆ ◆ ◆

The greatest honor that can come to a man is the appreciation and high regard of his fellowmen.   —H.G. Mendelson

◆ ◆ ◆

A foolish consistency is the hobgoblin of little minds, adored by little statesmen and philosophers and divines.
    —Ralph Waldo Emerson

Bing Crosby's favorite story of the spirit of the Irish concerns the memorable last words of his grandmother, Katie Harrigan. On her death bed, Katie said to her husband, who was sitting at her side, "Dennis, give me your hand."

Dennis placed his hand in hers and exclaimed dramatically, "Katie, it's a hand that was never raised against ye!"

Katie opened her eyes and glared at him.

"And it's a damn good thing for you it wasn't," she said. Then she closed her eyes and died happily.

♦ ♦ ♦

If you can command yourself, you can command the world.
—Chinese Proverb

♦ ♦ ♦

There is the greatest practical benefit in making a few failures early in life. —T.H. Huxley

♦ ♦ ♦

Until a boy has fallen in love, it's impossible to get him to shine his shoes.

♦ ♦ ♦

Anybody can be a good cook by using plenty of butter.

♦ ♦ ♦

Lack of cash is perhaps as strong a check on misbehavior as a strong will.

♦ ♦ ♦

Only when you have crossed the river can you say the crocodile has a lump on his snout. —African Proverb

Beauty on the outside never gets into the soul, but beauty of the soul reflects itself on the face. Its loveliness refuses to be imprisoned; it comes out on the eyes, the words, and the kindness of the hands.   —Bishop Fulton J. Sheen

♦ ♦ ♦

Introducing the guest speaker, the Master of Ceremonies listed his virtues in glowing terms.

"That introduction," grinned the guest, "reminds me of the man, who on judgment day, stuck his head out of the grave and read the epitaph on his headstone. 'Either somebody is a terrible liar, or I'm in the wrong hole.'"

♦ ♦ ♦

The nice thing about grandchildren is that you aren't too busy supporting them to have time to enjoy them.

♦ ♦ ♦

Jim Gittleson returned from a long-anticipated trip to Paris and was greeted by a friend.

"And how did you like Paris?" inquired the friend.

"Wonderful," replied Jim. "I just wish I could have made the trip twenty years ago."

"When Paris was really Paris, eh?" remarked the friend.

"No, when Jim Gittleson was really Jim Gittleson."

♦ ♦ ♦

I want nothing to do with natural foods. At my age I need all the preservatives I can get.   —George Burns

Leisure may prove to be a curse rather than a blessing, unless education teaches a flippant world that leisure is not a synonym for entertainment. —William J. Bogan

◆ ◆ ◆

A miser isn't much fun to live with, but he makes a wonderful ancestor.

◆ ◆ ◆

Help beautify our city dumps. Throw something pretty away today.

◆ ◆ ◆

The wife of an English professor entered his office to find his secretary on his lap. "George!" cried she, "I'm surprised!" "No, my dear," admonished the prof, "We are surprised. You are astounded."

◆ ◆ ◆

Adolescence is like a hitch in the Army—you'd hate to have missed it, and yet you'd hate to repeat it.

◆ ◆ ◆

What the superior man seeks is in himself.
What the mean man seeks is in others. —Confucius

◆ ◆ ◆

Regardless of how much money you have, wisdom has to be bought on the installment plan.

◆ ◆ ◆

Don't ask too much of any set of rules. Think of how long it is taking to put over the ones Moses presented. —David Bentham

◆ ◆ ◆

He does not believe that does not live according to his belief.
—Thomas Fuller

121

The clock of life is wound but once,
And no man has the power
   To tell just where the hands will stop,
At late or early hour.
   To lose one's wealth is sad indeed,
To lose one's health is more,
   To lose one's soul is such a loss
And no man can this restore.
   The present only is our own
Live, Love, Toil with a will
   Place no faith in "tomorrow"—for
The clock may then be still.

◆ ◆ ◆

Moderation is the silken string running through the pearl chain
of all virtues.   —Bishop Holt

◆ ◆ ◆

Hospital patient upon receiving his bill for an operation: "No
wonder they wore masks in the operating room."

◆ ◆ ◆

Waiting for some people to stop talking is like looking for the
end of a roller towel.

◆ ◆ ◆

The best afterdinner speech is when you hear, "Waiter, give me
both checks."

◆ ◆ ◆

One astrophysicist who travels widely has developed a theory to
explain the rings around Saturn. They are composed, he says, of
lost airline luggage.

122

It's pretty hard to find a pair of friends that is entirely satisfactory to both a man and his wife. —William Feather

♦ ♦ ♦

When you hear that a man is looking for you, and is very anxious to see you, it's something disagreeable.
—Edgar Watson Howe

♦ ♦ ♦

Reflect upon your present blessings, of which every man has plenty, not on your past misfortunes, of which all men have some.
—Charles Dickens

♦ ♦ ♦

When a husband opens the door and helps his wife into the car, it's safe to assume that he has just acquired one or the other.

♦ ♦ ♦

There is no fire like passion, there is no shark like hatred, there is no snare like folly, there is no torrent like greed. —Buddha

♦ ♦ ♦

South of the Equator, all climbing vines twine from right to left. North of the Equator they twine from left to right.

♦ ♦ ♦

Be glad of life because it gives you the chance to love and to work and to play and to look at the stars. —Henry Van Dyke

Lewis F. Powell, Justice, U.S. Supreme Court, retired: "The guarantee of a public trial was never intended to protect any right of the public to be entertained or even informed of current events. The purpose is to prevent secret trials."

♦ ♦ ♦

The advantage of leisure is mainly that we may have the power of choosing our own work, not certainly that it confers any privilege of idleness. —John Lubbock

♦ ♦ ♦

At the christening of her baby a mother asked the great general, Robert E. Lee, for some wisdom that would help her guide her son along the road to manhood. The general's immediate answer was: "Teach him to deny himself."

♦ ♦ ♦

Nothing makes a girl watch her figure so much as men who don't. —Franklin P. Jones

♦ ♦ ♦

Nothing can replace the modern swimsuit—and it has. —Joan I. Welsh

♦ ♦ ♦

Undoubtedly, the first man who ever tore a telephone book in half had a teen-aged daughter. —Joan I. Welsh

♦ ♦ ♦

Wise men profit more from fools than fools from wise men; for the wise men shun the mistakes of fools, but fools do not imitate the successes of the wise. —Cato

♦ ♦ ♦

After a feller gits famous it don't take long fer some one t' bob up that used t' set by him at school. —Kin Hubbard

September ushers in again
Autumn sun and autumn rain;
Bids the summer fond good-bye,
Hints at winter's frosty eye.
Yet with all its sad ado
September has its beauties too;
Radiant foliage, morning mist,
Air that serves as catalyst
To the changing season's train,
September days are here again.   —Jacques Ducharme

♦ ♦ ♦

Remember what the sergeant said to the recruit: "You might as well be happy here—no one here cares if you ain't."

♦ ♦ ♦

The man who trusts men will make fewer mistakes than he who distrusts them.   —Camillo Cavour

♦ ♦ ♦

Happy is the house that shelters a friend.
          —Ralph Waldo Emerson

♦ ♦ ♦

Amusement is the happiness of those who cannot think.
          —Alexander Pope

♦ ♦ ♦

Democracy is based upon the conviction that there are extraordinary possibilities in ordinary people.
          —Harry Emerson Fosdick

♦ ♦ ♦

'Twas founded be th' Puritans to give thanks f'r bein' presarved fr'm th' Indyans an' . . . we keep it to give thanks we are presarved fr'm th' Puritans.

AUTUMN

✦ THE LAW THE LAWYERS KNOW ABOUT

The law the lawyers know about
   Is property and land;
But why the leaves are on the trees,
And why the winds disturb the seas,
Why honey is the food of bees,
Why horses have such tender knees,
Why winters come and rivers freeze,
Why Faith is more than what one sees,
And Hope survives the worst disease,
And Charity is more than these,
   They do not understand.

—H.D.C. Pepler

♦ ♦ ♦

Folks who are everlastingly hard to please are never pleasant.

♦ ♦ ♦

Veni, vidi, Visa. (We came, we saw, we shopped.)

♦ ♦ ♦

Happiness is a direction, not a place.

♦ ♦ ♦

A theater critic I know told me that girls nowadays do things on stage they used to do off stage in order to get on stage.

♦ ♦ ♦

Middle age is that time of life when you don't care where your wife goes, just so you don't have to go along.

♦ ♦ ♦

Money doesn't talk these days—it goes without saying.

You don't get rich in politics unless you are a crook.
—Harry Truman

◆ ◆ ◆

It's nice to know that the nation's racetracks are holding the line against inflation. The $2 betting window is still $2.

◆ ◆ ◆

Some stretch pants have no other choice.

◆ ◆ ◆

If you think nobody cares if you're alive, try missing a couple of car payments.

◆ ◆ ◆

On his tenth anniversary, a bandleader who had played over 3,000 dance dates was asked, "What have you had the most requests for?"
Replied the bandleader, "Where's the men's room?"

◆ ◆ ◆

Better to remain silent and be thought a fool than to speak and to remove all doubt.
—Abraham Lincoln

◆ ◆ ◆

He didn't carve his career—he chiseled it.   —Walter Winchell

◆ ◆ ◆

Look before you leap, for snakes among sweet flowers do creep.
—Old Proverb

◆ ◆ ◆

The more a man possesses over and above what he uses, the more careworn he becomes.
—George Bernard Shaw

The frontier between hell and heaven is only the difference between two ways of looking at things.　—George Bernard Shaw

♦ ♦ ♦

Let us endeavor so to live that when we come to die even the undertaker will be sorry.　　　　　　　　　　—Mark Twain

♦ ♦ ♦

It is indeed desirable to be well descended, but the glory belongs to our ancestors.　　　　　　　　　　—Plutarch

♦ ♦ ♦

✸ When a friend deals with a friend, let the bargain be clear and well-penned that they may continue friends to the end.
　　　　　　　　　　　　　　　　　　—Benjamin Franklin

♦ ♦ ♦

The average man thinks lawyers are dishonest because if he were a lawyer he would be dishonest.
　　　　　　　　　　　　　—Attributed to William A. Blatt

♦ ♦ ♦

✸It's pretty hard for any of us to go through this world without either increasing or diminishing somebody's happiness.
　　　　　　　　　　　　　　　　　　—P.K. Sideliner

♦ ♦ ♦

Hope is generally a wrong guide, though it is very good company by the way.　　　　　　　　　　—George Savile

♦ ♦ ♦

He that would eat the fruit must climb the tree. —James Kelley

♦ ♦ ♦

There is always free cheese in a mouse trap.

Autumn is The war between summer + winter. MH9B

Delicious Autumn! My very soul is wedded to it, and if I were a ✸
bird I would fly about the earth seeking the successive autumns.
—George Eliot

◆ ◆ ◆

Before deciding to retire, stay home for a week and watch the
daytime TV shows. —Bill Copeland

◆ ◆ ◆

It is possible for one to tell you all the facts and still not all the
truth.

◆ ◆ ◆

Mother Nature is providential. She gives us twelve years to
develop a love for our children before turning them into teenagers.
—Eugene P. Bertin

◆ ◆ ◆

When asked what lesson he had learned from civilization, an
old Indian replied: "Ingratitude."

◆ ◆ ◆

You traverse the world in search of happiness, which is within
the reach of every man; a contented mind confers it all.
—Horace

◆ ◆ ◆

Books are the quietest and most constant of friends; they are the
most accessible and wisest of counselors, and the most patient of
teachers. —Charles W. Eliot

Go to friends for advice;
To women for pity;
To strangers for charity;
To relatives for nothing.   —Spanish Proverb

♦ ♦ ♦

The fashion wears out more apparel than the man.
                                    —William Shakespeare

♦ ♦ ♦

A boy is, of all wild beasts, the most difficult to manage.
                                                    —Plato

♦ ♦ ♦

"What's your son going to be when he finally graduates from college?"
"Senile."

♦ ♦ ♦

Sign in a New York cafeteria window: "Courteous and efficient self-service."

♦ ♦ ♦

A lot of people don't realize they have an identity crisis until they try to cash a check in a strange town.

♦ ♦ ♦

✚ Where no counsel is, the people fall: but in the multitude of counselors there is safety.   —Solomon

♦ ♦ ♦

The goods which please are already half sold.
                                        —French Proverb

Fire and Ice . . . ❧

Some say the world will end in fire,
Some say in ice.
From what I've tasted of desire
I hold with those who favor fire.
But if it had to perish twice,
I think I know enough of hate
To say that for destruction ice
Is also great
And would suffice.   —Robert Frost

♦ ♦ ♦

During noon recess of a case in Rock Island, Lincoln walked
out to the railroad bridge and came to a boy sitting on the end of a
tie with a fishing pole out over the water. And Lincoln, fresh from
the squabbles and challenges of the courtroom, said to the boy,
"Well, I suppose you know all about this river."
Said the boy, "Sure, mister, it was here before I was born and
it's been here ever since."
Lincoln smiled, "Well, it's good to be out here where there is so
much fact and so little opinion."

♦ ♦ ♦

Know more than others if you can, but do not tell them so. ✳
                          —Earl of Chesterfield

♦ ♦ ♦

Man is the only creature that dares to light a fire and to live with
it. The reason? Because he alone has learned how to put it out.
                          —Henry Van Dyke

133

When we questioned a newspaper writer's statement that he lived well on $12 a week in 1936, a West Virginia reader consulted a memorandum book in which he records daily expenditures, and noted some of the prices in 1939:

Milk (quart), 10 cents; wine (5th), 35 cents; sausage (2 pounds), 25 cents; soap, 5 cents; moving picture show, 25 cents; pork chops (pound), 25 cents; celery (bunch), 5 cents; bread, 5 cents; bran flakes, 10 cents; lunch, 25 cents; shortening (5 pounds), 50 cents; oysters (pint), 22 cents; butter, 30 cents; prunes (3 pounds), 20 cents; purchased a good shirt for 69 cents; bought a turkey for a dollar; hair-cut was 50 cents; jello (4 packs), 15 cents; candy was 10 cents a pound; oranges (10 pounds), 29 cents; grapes (pound), 10 cents; a package of mince meat was 12 cents; can of cranberry sauce, 12 cents; can of peaches, 13 cents; applesauce (4 cans), 25 cents.

I am glad I have a short memory; otherwise these comparisons would be too, too disturbing.   *—Beckett Newsletter*

◆ ◆ ◆

It is a part of the American character to consider nothing as desperate.   —Thomas Jefferson

◆ ◆ ◆

If a man be endowed with a generous mind, this is the best kind of nobility.   —Plato

◆ ◆ ◆

Egotist—A person of low taste, more interested in himself than in me.   —Ambrose Bierce

◆ ◆ ◆

Bore, n. a person who talks when you wish him to listen.
                                        —Ambrose Bierce

Epitaph on a stone raised to four wives, their ashes in four urns that had been overturned in a gale, Kent, England:

Stranger pause
And shed a tear:
For Mary Jane
Lies Buried Here
Mingled in a most
Surprising manner
With Susan, Joy
And portions of Hanna.

From Topsfield, Mass., on Mary Lefavour, who died in 1797, age 74:

Reader pass on and ne'er waste your time,
On bad biography and bitter rhyme
For what I am this cumb'rous clay insures,
And what I was, is no affair of yours.

On Jonathan Fiddle from Hartscombe, England:

On the 22nd of June
Jonathan Fiddle
Went out of tune.

♦ ♦ ♦

The easiest way to live within your means is partly.
—Franklin P. Jones

♦ ♦ ♦

Even when the experts all agree, they may well be mistaken.
—Bertrand Russell, Earl Russell

♦ ♦ ♦

It is a kind of spiritual snobbery that makes people think they can be happy without money.   —Albert Camus

October . . .

When the weeds by the roadside are colored with yellow
The fruit of the fields is ripened and mellow
The leaves on the trees are gloriously red
With a wonderful blue sky over your head.
When with silver grey smoke each valley is filled
And the air is like wine deliciously chilled
You know without naming the season or days
It's the month of October you see through the haze.
                                                    —Alma Hahn

♦ ♦ ♦

More Epitaphs . . .

On Ezekiel Pease in Nantucket, Mass.:
        He is not here
        But only his pod:
        He shelled out his peas
        And went to his God.

♦ ♦ ♦

There is only one thing in the world worse than being talked
about, and that is not being talked about.   —Oscar Wilde

♦ ♦ ♦

A homeowner wearing his oldest clothes, was cutting the lawn
when a woman in a brand new car stopped and shouted:
    "What do you get for doing yard work?"
The owner looked back at the house and then at the woman.
"The lady of the house lets me sleep with her," he said.

136

In 1784, Benjamin Franklin wrote the following letter to Benjamin Webb:

"Dear Sir: Your situation grieves me and I send you herewith a banknote for ten louis d'or. I do not pretend to give such a sum; I only lend it to you. When you shall return to your country, you cannot fail of getting into some business that will in time enable you to pay all your debts. In that case, when you meet with another honest man in similar distress, you must pay me by lending the sum to him, enjoining him to discharge the debt by a like operation when he shall be able and shall meet with such another opportunity. I hope it may thus go through many hands before it meets with a knave that will stop its progress. This is a trick of mine for doing a deal of good with a little money. I am not rich enough to afford much in good works, and so am obliged to be cunning and make the most of a little. With best wishes for your future prosperity, I am, dear sir, you most obedient servant.

—Benjamin Franklin"

◆ ◆ ◆

Hating people is like burning down your own house to get rid of a rat.   —Harry Emerson Fosdick

◆ ◆ ◆

Do good to thy friend to keep him, to thy enemy to gain him.
—Benjamin Franklin

◆ ◆ ◆

If, in instructing a child, you are vexed with it for want of adroitness, try, if you have never tried before, to write with your left hand, and then remember that a child is all left hand.
—J.F. Boyse

◆ ◆ ◆

A small college at an athletic meet had a cross-eyed javelin thrower—he didn't win any medals but he sure kept the crowd alert.

137

Did you know . . . that every queen named Jane has either been murdered, imprisoned, gone mad, died young, or been dethroned?

That's one of the unique facts unearthed by David Louis in his book *2201 Fascinating Facts* (Crown Publishers).

Here are others:

You can escape a pursuing crocodile by running in zigzag fashion. Crocodiles are surprisingly fast, but they cannot suddenly change direction.

Roman statues had detachable heads so they could be replaced.

Kilts are native to France, not Scotland.

Inventor Thomas Edison and authors Noel Coward, Charles Dickens, and Mark Twain never graduated from grade school.

The Greek national anthem has 158 verses.

The Apollo landings caused the moon's surface to vibrate for 55 minutes.

You can buy playing cards for left-handed people.

The deer botfly can fly at 818 mph—faster than a jet.

◆ ◆ ◆

The test of every religious, political, or educational system is the man it forms.
— Henri-Frédéric Amiel

◆ ◆ ◆

If each hung up his pack of troubles on a wall and looked around at the troubles of others, he would quickly run to grab his own pack of troubles.
— Yiddish Proverb

◆ ◆ ◆

An expert doesn't necessarily know more than anyone else. He just has it better organized and he uses slides!
— Bill Coplin

◆ ◆ ◆

Some of us do not believe we are having a good time unless we are doing something we can't afford.

138

Something Told the Wild Geese

Something told the wild geese
It was time to go,
Though the fields lay golden
Something whispered, "Snow."
Leaves were green and stirring.
Berries, luster-glossed,
But beneath warm feathers
Something cautioned, "Frost."
All the sagging orchards
Steamed with amber spice,
But each wild breast stiffened
At remembered ice.
Something told the wild geese
It was time to fly—
Summer sun was on their wings,
Winter in their cry.

                           —Rachel Field

♦ ♦ ♦

He who has injured thee was either stronger or weaker than thee. If weaker, spare him; if stronger, spare thyself.   —Seneca

♦ ♦ ♦

To get back to sirloin for a moment, do you know how this cut of beef got its name? One of the more interesting origins tells of King James I of England stopping at an inn in Lancashire. While there, the host provided a magnificent loin of beef. The King was so impressed that he drew his sword and knighted the remnants of the beef—Sir Loin.   —The IN Box, Aetna Life & Casualty

♦ ♦ ♦

There's a divinity that shapes our ends,
Rough-hew them how we will.   —William Shakespeare

The morns are meeker than they were,
The nuts are getting brown;
The berry's cheek is plumper,
The rose is out of town.
The maple wears a gayer scarf,
The field a scarlet gown.
Lest I should be old-fashioned,
I'll put a trinket on.   —Emily Dickinson

♦ ♦ ♦

❋ Make a joyful noise unto the Lord, all ye lands.

Serve the Lord with gladness: come before his presence with singing.

Know ye that the Lord he *is* God: *it is* he *that* hath made us, and not we ourselves; *we are* his people, and the sheep of his pasture.

Enter into his gates with thanksgiving, *and* into his courts with praise: be thankful unto him, *and* bless his name.

For the Lord *is* good, his mercy is everlasting; and his truth *endureth* to all generations.   —Psalm 100

♦ ♦ ♦

Think what you do when you run in debt; you give to another power over your liberty. If you cannot pay at the time, you will be ashamed to see your creditor. . . . It is hard for an empty bag to stand upright.   —Benjamin Franklin

♦ ♦ ♦

A tourist was making his first visit to the national capitol, and a friendly cab driver was driving him around to see the beautiful buildings. As they rode past the government archives building, the tourist noticed the carved words across the huge building. "What Is Past Is Prologue."

"Just what does that mean?" the tourist asked.

"It means," said the driver, "that you ain't seen nothin' yet."

How Do I Love Thee? . . .

How do I love thee? Let me count the ways.
I love thee to the depth and breadth and height
My soul can reach, when feeling out of sight
For the ends of Being and ideal Grace.
I love thee to the level of everyday's
Most quiet need, by sun and candle-light.
I love thee freely, as men strive for Right;
I love thee purely, as they turn from Praise.
I love thee with the passion put to use
In my old griefs, and with my childhood's faith.
I love thee with a love I seemed to lose
With my lost saints,—I love thee with the breath,
Smiles, tears, of all my life!—and, if God choose,
I shall but love thee better after death.
                              —Elizabeth Barrett Browning

♦ ♦ ♦

The best kind of sex education is life in a loving family.
                              —Rosemary Haughton

♦ ♦ ♦

Friend—"Why have you the General in such a peculiar pose?"
Sculptor—"You see, it was started as an equestrian statue, and
then the committee found they couldn't afford the horse."

♦ ♦ ♦

A college education never hurt anyone willing to learn something afterwards.

♦ ♦ ♦

Deal with the faults of others as gently as with your own.
                              —Chinese Proverb

141

Senator Everett Dirksen tells of overhearing two men talking on a hotel porch in eastern Tennessee.

"It's your life," the first man began, "but you smoke entirely too much. How many cigars do you smoke a day?"

"About 10 a day for the past 30 years."

"And what do you pay for them?"

"Fifty cents."

"Think of that," the first exclaimed. "That's five dollars a day and over 30 years would be almost 55 thousand dollars. Why, you could own this hotel if you'd have saved that much by not smoking."

"Do you own the hotel?" the second man asked.

"No."

"Well, I do."

♦ ♦ ♦

What seems so necessary today may not even be desirable tomorrow.

♦ ♦ ♦

The modern girl wears just as many clothes as her grandma, but not all at the same time.　　　　　　　　　　—Sam Levenson

♦ ♦ ♦

He who has never learned to be courteous must always be on the hunt for new customers.　　　　　　　　　　—C.F. Norton

♦ ♦ ♦

Though we travel the world over to find the beautiful, we must carry it with us or we find it not.　　　—Ralph Waldo Emerson

142

A young lad was being tested for glasses, but he couldn't focus his eyes on the chart, and the optometrist was having a hard time. Finally he took a paper bag, cut two eye holes in it and placed it over the boy's head. "Now tell me what you can see," he requested. The boy began to cry.

"What's the matter?" the optometrist asked.

"I want wire rims like my brother's" sobbed the boy.

◆ ◆ ◆

I have no pleasure in any man who despises music. It is no invention of ours: it is the gift of God. I place it next to theology. Satan hates music: he knows how it drives the evil spirit out of us.

—Martin Luther

◆ ◆ ◆

A Sunday-school teacher who had been a victim of difficulties in motivating her 8-year-old charges decided to try a new technique with the story of the Good Samaritan. In introducing the story, she pointed her finger at one of the least attentive and asked the following:

"Suppose you were walking down the street and suddenly saw a man lying in a vacant lot in ragged clothes. Suppose he was dirty and covered with blood from a beating he had received. What would you do?"

The response was "I'd throw up!"

◆ ◆ ◆

Why can't life's problems hit us when we're 17 and know everything? —A.C. Jolly

◆ ◆ ◆

With years a richer life begins,
    The spirit mellows:
Ripe age gives tone to violins,
    Wine, and good fellows.
                —John Trowbridge

Sir Richard Pim, who was in charge of Winston Churchill's map room during World War II, reported that on the day of the election which removed the prime minister from office in 1945, he went into Churchill's bath to tell him of the unfavorable trend of returns. He quoted Churchill as saying: "They have a perfect right to kick us out. That is democracy. That's what we have been fighting for. Please hand me my towel."

♦ ♦ ♦

Things don't change, but by and by our wishes change.
—Marcel Proust

♦ ♦ ♦

Charles L. Drake, oceanographer for Lamont Geological Laboratory at Columbia University, telling of the first efforts to scan the bottom of the sea: "It was frustrating. The first thing we saw down there was a beer bottle."

♦ ♦ ♦

The youngster had gone on his first long camping trip with the Boy Scouts. His doting mother anxiously asked him whether he had become homesick.

"Nope," he replied. "The only kids who got homesick were the ones with dogs back home."

♦ ♦ ♦

Tolerance is the positive and cordial effort to understand another's beliefs, practices and habits without necessarily sharing or accepting them.
—Joshua L. Liebman

144

There is an old Jewish legend about the origin of praise. After God created mankind, says the legend, He asked the angels what they thought of the world He had made. "Only one thing is lacking," they said. "It is the sound of praise to the Creator." So, the story continues, "God created music, the voice of birds, the whispering wind, the murmuring ocean, and planted melody in the hearts of men."

◆ ◆ ◆

Church records a century and a half old remind us how much the world has changed. In one little Ohio town, the local church elected two officers whose titles seem strange today—"Pointer" and "Beaner." The duties of the Pointer were to point out, by calling their names, those in the congregation who should take note of some point made in the sermon. The Beaner had the job which would delight even a grade-schooler of today. He sat in the choir loft with a beanshot and watched for drowsy parishioners whom he promptly awakened. It is assumed, of course, that his aim was excellent.

◆ ◆ ◆

Little Johnny announced to his grocer that there was a new baby at his home. "Is he going to stay?" the grocer asked.

"I guess so," replied Johnny, "he's got all his things off."

◆ ◆ ◆

A woman had given herself a fancy new permanent wave. Two of her neighbors were discussing the job after they had seen the results of her new efforts. "What do you think of it?" asked the first.

"Well, if you ask me," said the second, "it looks like her parole came through just as the warden pulled the switch."

Fourth graders in one of New York City's schools for gifted children were asked to complete a sentence beginning: "Let's be as quiet as . . ."

Some of the answers, as reported in the *New York Times:* ". . . a leaf turning colors;" ". . . a feather falling from a bird;" ". . . time passing;" ". . . the first star coming out;" ". . . the sun coming up in the morning;" ". . . children sleeping;" ". . . when you pray;" ". . . a butterfly flying."

♦ ♦ ♦

At a revival meeting, the preacher talked about virtue and goodness and wound up his sermon by saying, "No one really likes sin. Will everyone who likes sin please stand up?"

Of course, everyone in the congregation remained seated—except one old man, wearing a hearing aid, in the rear of the auditorium.

"You like sin, brother?" asked the astounded preacher.

"No," the man replied disgustedly, "I thought you said gin!"

♦ ♦ ♦

After receiving $10, the fortune teller informed her patron that he was entitled to ask two questions.

"But isn't that a great deal of money for just two questions?" the man asked.

"It is," acknowledged the fortune teller. "Now, your second question . . . ?"

♦ ♦ ♦

Truth is tough. It will not break like a bubble, at a touch; nay, you may kick it about all day, like a football, and it will be round and full at evening.   —Oliver Wendell Holmes, Jr.

146

Love of Country . . .

Breathes there the man, with soul so dead,
Who never to himself hath said,
This is my own, my native land!
Whose heart hath ne'er within him burned
As home his footsteps he hath turned
From wandering on a foreign strand!
If such there breathe, go mark him well;
For him no Minstrel raptures swell;
High though his titles, proud his name,
Boundless his wealth as wish can claim;
Despite those titles, power, and pelf,
The wretch, concentered all in self,
Living, shall forfeit fair renown,
And, doubly dying, shall go down
To the vile dust, from whence he sprung,
Unwept, unhonored, and unsung.   —Sir Walter Scott

◆ ◆ ◆

The first-grader was talking about the recent fire in his school.
"I knew it was going to happen," he said. "We had been practicing for it all year."

◆ ◆ ◆

I have always considered applause at the beginning of a lecture a
manifestation of faith. If it comes in the middle, it is a sign of
hope. And if it comes at the end, it is always charity.
      —Rabbi Abraham R. Besdin

◆ ◆ ◆

If I were asked . . . to what the singular prosperity and growing
strength of that people [the Americans] ought mainly to be attributed, I should reply: To the superiority of their women.
      —Alexis de Tocqueville

A Vagabond Song . . .

There is something in the autumn that is native to my blood—
Touch of manner, hint of mood;
And my heart is like a rhyme,
With the yellow and the purple and the crimson keeping time.
The scarlet of the maples can shake me like a cry
Of bugles going by.
And my lonely spirit thrills
To see the frosty asters like a smoke upon the hills.
There is something in October sets the gypsy blood astir;
We must rise and follow her,
When from every hill of flame
She calls and calls each vagabond by name.   —Bliss Carman

♦ ♦ ♦

Some idea of inflation comes from seeing a youngster get his first job at a salary you dreamed of as the culmination of your career.

♦ ♦ ♦

Once upon a time a father read that a middle-aged man should not shovel wet snow because he could have a heart attack. So he called in his teenager and said, "Son, a middle-aged man should not shovel wet snow because he could have a heart attack. So would you do it for me?" The son said "yes." And the father had a heart attack.

♦ ♦ ♦

A small town is where you deserve less credit for resisting temptation than for finding it.

148

The International boundary between the United States proper and the Dominion of Canada has a total length of 3,987 miles, about 1,749 miles of this being over land and 2,238 over water. The land part is marked variously with monuments of iron, aluminum-bronze set on concrete, stone cairns, and concrete, placed at points ranging from two and a half to four miles apart. Most of the rock and earth mounds, once common on the international boundary, have been replaced by metal monuments. A vista has been cut through the trees where the line runs over wooded areas. . . . The boundary between Alaska and Canada is 1,538 miles long and is indicated by monuments of concrete, aluminum-bronze, conical shaped piles of stone, and brass bolts. Thus it will be seen that the combined common boundary between United States and Canadian territory has an extent of about 5,525 miles. It is marked with 8,060 monuments of various kinds and has the distinction of being the longest demilitarized boundary in the world between two nations, there being no fort, warship, military force, or other armament of defense along the entire stretch.

◆ ◆ ◆

The young son of the big business man visited his office one day.

"Daddy, what do you do here all day long?"

"Oh, nothing much," said the big business man.

"Well, then, how do you know when you are done?" pursued the youngster.

◆ ◆ ◆

During a heated debate in the U.S. Senate, one man told another to "go to h---." The Senator so attacked appealed to the Vice President, Calvin Coolidge, who was presiding, concerning the propriety of the remark.

Coolidge, who had been idly leafing through a book, looked up and said, "I've been going through the rule book. You don't have to go."

My good blade carves the casques of men,
My tough lance thrusteth sure,
My strength is as the strength of ten,
Because my heart is pure.   —Alfred, Lord Tennyson

♦ ♦ ♦

The most idiotic thing anyone can do is to take up a hobby. The hobby must take him up.   —Albert P. Terhune

♦ ♦ ♦

The click of the knitting needles, the creak of the rocker, and the ticking of the grandfather's clock were all that disturbed the silence of the warm, sunny room. With childish curiosity little Gloria sat watching the purls and stitches.

"Grandma," she asked, "why do you knit?"

"Oh," wheezed the old lady, "just for the hell of it."

♦ ♦ ♦

Laughter is God's hand upon a troubled world.   —Zazu Pitts

♦ ♦ ♦

In England, after the stagecoaches were started, writers condemned the new method of travel. "These coaches," they said, "make country gentlemen come to London on small occasion, which otherwise they would not do but on urgent necessity; nay, the conveniency of the passage makes their wives come up, who, rather than make such long journeys on horseback would stay at home. Here, when they come to town, they must be in fashion, get fine clothes, and by this means get such a habit of idleness and love of pleasure that they are uneasy ever after."

If everyone swept in front of his house, the whole town would be clean.   —Polish Proverb

♦ ♦ ♦

Dorothy Parker once collided with Claire Boothe Luce in a narrow doorway. "Age before beauty," said Mrs. Luce, stepping aside. "Pearls before swine," said Dorothy Parker, gliding through.

♦ ♦ ♦

Only six of the fifty-six signers of the Declaration of Independence were subsequently among the thirty-nine signers of the original draft of the Federal Constitution. Four of these six— Benjamin Franklin, Robert Morris, James Wilson, and George Clymer—were from Pennsylvania. The other two were Roger Sherman, of Connecticut, and George Read, of Delaware.

♦ ♦ ♦

Diligence is the mother of good luck, and God gives all things to industry. Then plough deep while sluggards sleep, and you shall have corn to sell and to keep.   —Benjamin Franklin

♦ ♦ ♦

Market Tips Translated—
    "Somewhat speculative issue." (You call it. Heads or tails?)
    "Has great growth potential." (Hasn't done a thing so far.)
    "Expects a very favorable earnings report." (Too bad you weren't on the bandwagon a year ago.)
    "A strong institutional favorite." (A run-of-the-mill utility.)
    "Now trading at more realistic levels." (Now selling below what you paid for it.)

151

The seat of the Lord Chancellor of England in the House of Lords consists of a large, rectangular bag of wool covered with red cloth. It resembles a cushioned ottoman or divan, without back or arms, and stands almost in the center of the hall in front of the magnificent and canopied thrones of the King and Queen. During the reign of Elizabeth, when wool was one of England's chief sources of wealth, Parliament passed an act prohibiting the exportation of that commodity. At that time the high judges of the realm were provided with sacks of wool as seats so that they might be constantly reminded of the English woolen industry. The Lord Chancellor, who is head of the chancery division of the high court of justice, presides over the House of Lords, and his seat is to this day a woolsack.

◆ ◆ ◆

A hotel manager in Los Angeles called on an art dealer and asked to see watercolors to go into his renovated rooms. After turning down several prints, he said:

"I don't care about the subjects . . . or the artist. Just show me pictures that are too large to fit into a suitcase."

◆ ◆ ◆

Some folks won't ask for advice for fear of giving the impression they need it.

◆ ◆ ◆

TV has come a long way. First it was black and white. Then it was color. Now it's off-color.

◆ ◆ ◆

"Darling, I've missed you," said the wife,
   With much emotion, then,
She fixed her gaze upon his form,
   And fired the gun again!

—F.G. Kernan

152

The curfew tolls the knell of parting day,
The lowing herd wind slowly o'er the lea,
The plowman homeward plods his weary way,
And leaves the world to darkness and to me.

Beneath those rugged elms, that yew tree's shade,
Where heaves the turf in many a moldering heap,
Each in his narrow cell forever laid,
The rude forefathers of the hamlet sleep.

Far from the madding crowd's ignoble strife,
Their sober wishes never learned to stray;
Along the cool sequester'd vale of life
They kept the noiseless tenor of their way.　　—Thomas Gray

♦ ♦ ♦

Each time I look at a fine landscape:
Each time that I meet a loved friend,
I raise my voice and recite a stanza of poetry
And am glad as though a God had crossed my path.　　—Po Chui

♦ ♦ ♦

I was never less alone than when with myself.
　　　　　　　　　　　　　—Edward Gibbon

♦ ♦ ♦

　　A grasshopper walked into a tavern and hopped up on the bar
stool. He said to the bartender, "I'll have a Scotch and soda."
　　The bartender said, "Did you know we have a drink named
after you?"
　　"Really, you mean you have a drink named Irving?"

153

Scheduled for a speech? Don't eat during the two hours before you're scheduled on the podium. If you are at a banquet, simply toy with your food.

If hunger compels you to eat, stick to an opera star's all-protein diet. Milk products and sweets coat your tongue and larnyx, and double the saliva in your mouth.

Keep the speech short, 20 minutes or less. The mind can absorb only what the seat can endure.

Never close with "Thank you"; it's an admission of failure. If the speech was a good one, the audience should thank you.

—Maxeda Von Hesse

♦ ♦ ♦

As a general rule, nobody has money who ought to have it.

—Benjamin Disraeli

♦ ♦ ♦

A man who will believe only what he can understand must have either a long head or a short creed. —Oliver Wendell Holmes

♦ ♦ ♦

A widow is the luckiest woman in the world. She knows all about men and all the men who know anything about her are dead.

—*The Lyman Letter*

♦ ♦ ♦

A group of kindergarten children visited the local police station and viewed the pictures of the 10 most wanted men.

One child pointed to a picture and asked if it really was the photograph of the wanted person. "Yes," answered the policeman guide.

"Well," inquired the youngster, "Why didn't you keep him when you took his picture?" —*Rotary Club Bulletin*

When love and skill work together expect a masterpiece.

—John Ruskin

♦ ♦ ♦

George Cheyne, a Scottish physician, when a person was talking about the excellence of human nature, exclaimed:

"Hoot, hoot, man! Human nature is a rogue and a scoundrel, or why should it perpetually stand in need of laws and of religion?"

♦ ♦ ♦

There is a pleasure in the pathless woods,
There is a rapture on the lonely shore,
There is society, where none intrudes,
By the deep sea, and music in its roar:
I love not man the less, but Nature more.   —Lord Byron

♦ ♦ ♦

It requires greater virtues to support good fortune than bad.

—Francois, Duc de La Rochefoucauld

♦ ♦ ♦

Content makes poor men rich; Discontent makes rich men poor.

—Benjamin Franklin

♦ ♦ ♦

The development of a new product is a three-step process: first, an American firm announces an invention; second, the Russians claim they made the same discovery twenty years ago; third, the Japanese start exporting it.

"And remember," said the boss, "your salary is personal and should not be discussed with anyone."

"Oh, don't worry, sir. I'm just as ashamed of it as you are."

♦ ♦ ♦

An old farmer and his wife were leaning on their pigsty when the old lady wistfully murmured, "Tomorrow's our golden wedding anniversary, John. Let's kill the pig."

The farmer pondered the suggestion, removed a stray straw from his sleeve, and wearily replied, "What's the use of murdering the pig for what happened 50 years ago?"

♦ ♦ ♦

Bank accounts give a person a good feeling . . . until he realizes they are insured by an agency of a Federal government that's two trillion dollars in debt.   *—The Indianapolis News*

♦ ♦ ♦

A key chain is a gadget that allows us to lose several keys at the same time.

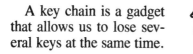

♦ ♦ ♦

The worst thing about going into business for yourself is that it takes the fun out of payday.

♦ ♦ ♦

The U.S. once had a state named Franklin but it lasted only four years. The State of Franklin became part of eastern Tennessee in 1788.

In 1789, it took George Washington eight days to travel the 200-odd miles from his home, Mount Vernon, to the scene of his inauguration as President in New York City. The fact that it required eight days is not significant. The important fact is that the time was the same as it would have taken 2,000 years before. No real progress had been made in transportation in twenty centuries. Moses or Nebuchadnezzar could have traveled just as rapidly. Julius Caesar could have stepped from the first century into the nineteenth more easily than Benjamin Franklin could have stepped into 1976. Now for the first time in history, no man dies in the historical epoch in which he was born.

◆ ◆ ◆

Certainly Columbus was the world's most remarkable salesman. He started out not knowing where he was going. When he got there, he didn't know where he was. And when he got back, he didn't know where he had been. And he did it all on a big cash advance, and he got a repeat order.

◆ ◆ ◆

A friend was very upset at having to get rid of his cat. Dorothy Parker suggested, "Have you tried curiosity?"

◆ ◆ ◆

All great deeds and all great thoughts have a ridiculous beginning. Great works are often born on a street corner or in a restaurant's revolving door. —Albert Camus

157

By this time, most of the population of the United States has either read Frank Baum's *The Wizard of Oz* or seen it on TV—or both. Yet it's a safe bet that few people know where the name "Oz" came from. According to the late author's own autobiography, he had outlined the story of Dorothy and the Tin Man and the Straw Man and the Cowardly Lion and all the others in his mind, but still had not hit upon a name for the magic land they were seeking, when his eyes fell on a filing cabinet in a corner of his office. The top drawer of his file was labeled "A-H," the second drawer, "I-N" and the bottom drawer, "O-Z." "That's it!" he cried delightedly. "OZ!"

♦ ♦ ♦

Anybody who thinks there must be fire when there's smoke has never tried burning autumn leaves.

♦ ♦ ♦

Experience is the thing that enables you to recognize a mistake when you make it again.

♦ ♦ ♦

Nothing makes it easier to resist temptation than a proper upbringing, a sound set of values, and witnesses.
—Franklin P. Jones

♦ ♦ ♦

Love is to the moral nature what the sun is to the earth.
—Honoré de Balzac

Every great achievement was once *impossible.*

♦ ♦ ♦

You raise your voice when you should reinforce your argument.
—Samuel Johnson

♦ ♦ ♦

Apathy is one of America's greatest problems—but who cares?

♦ ♦ ♦

The real state of a polite person is to have the same ailment the other person is describing and not mention it.

♦ ♦ ♦

I've never said I was the best singer in the world. There are better singers than me around—Sinatra and Tony Bennett—and that's about it.   —George Burns

♦ ♦ ♦

A small stuffed gorilla in a museum had begun to look a bit shabby and the museum engaged a taxidermist to recondition the animal. The taxidermist took the gorilla to his shop, finishing the job the next evening. So he put the gorilla in the back seat of his car and was returning it to the museum when a cop pulled him over for speeding.

While writing out the ticket, the cop delivered the usual lecture. He then peered into the gloomy interior of the car. "Who's that?" he barked, shuddering visibly.

"Oh, her?" The taxidermist was not without a sense of humor. "Why, that's my wife."

Slowly the cop began tearing up the ticket. "Drive on, fella," he whispered, "you've got trouble enough."

The Night Has a Thousand Eyes . .

The night has a thousand eyes,
And the day but one;
Yet the light of the bright world dies
With the dying sun.
The mind has a thousand eyes,
And the heart but one;
Yet the light of a whole life dies
When love is done.   —Francis William Bourdillon

♦ ♦ ♦

Deceiving my wife is like trying to sneak a sunrise past a
rooster.   —Roy Hatten

♦ ♦ ♦

The excited young father wanted to do everything just right. As
he was about to leave the hospital with his wife and newborn son,
he asked the doctor, "What time should we wake the little fellow
in the morning?"

♦ ♦ ♦

Better keep yourself clean and bright; you are the window
through which you must see the world.   —George Bernard Shaw

♦ ♦ ♦

If the stars should appear one night in a thousand years, how
would men believe and adore!   —Ralph Waldo Emerson

♦ ♦ ♦

The vanity of being trusted with a secret is generally one of the
chief motives to disclose it.   —Samuel Johnson

♦ ♦ ♦

A football fan is a guy who yells at the quarterback for not being
able to pinpoint a receiver 46 yards downfield, and then can't even
find his own car in the parking lot after the game.

September . . .

Chill hands of death on Summer's brow are laid;
Cool, calm, serene she lies, all unafraid
Of Death. Her task's complete,
Her bounteous store is laid at the tired feet
Of those who toiled. Take her bequest.
Midst Autumn's dancing leaves lay her to rest,
Rejoicing. For through God's evolving plan,
Our summers all come back to us again.   —Rolland R. Otis

♦ ♦ ♦

A tightwad went into a gift shop to find an inexpensive gift for a friend but he found everything very expensive until he spotted a vase that had been broken. He purchased it for practically nothing and asked the store to send it. He wanted the friend to think it was broken in transit.

A week later he received a thank you note. It read, "Many thanks for the vase. It was nice of you to wrap each piece separately."

♦ ♦ ♦

Tots who started kindergarten at a certain elementary school came home the first day with a special note for mom from the teacher which read, in part: "If you promise not to believe everything your child says happens at school, I'll promise not to believe everything he says happens at home."

♦ ♦ ♦

If you have something to do that is worthwhile, don't talk about it—do it. After you've done it your friends will talk about it.

161

Animal/vegetable—
Cell on cell the same.
Split a living tissue:
   Molecular structure
   Each again the same.
Observe the plan, the grand design
   Of all that lives
   And dies to further life.
What hint of heaven in the heavens:
   With galaxies of light,
   Countless patterns of eternity?
All this and more an accident
   Without cause and reason
   For lack of proof?
Hardly . . .

♦ ♦ ♦

He bought a new shirt, and on a slip pinned to the inside found the name and address of a girl with the words: Please write and send a photograph.

"Ah," he said, "here is romance."

He wrote to the girl and sent a picture of himself. In due course an answer came, and with a heart aflutter, he opened it. It was only a note reading: I was just curious to see what kind of fellow would wear such a funny shirt.

♦ ♦ ♦

I've taken care of myself all my life. I have never shed a tear over a guy; they ain't worth it.   —Mae West

♦ ♦ ♦

I'm a slow walker, but I never walk back.   —Abraham Lincoln

162

Honest labor bears a lovely face. —Thomas Dekker

♦ ♦ ♦

The surest cure for vanity is loneliness. —Thomas Wolfe

♦ ♦ ♦

What can the enemy do when the friend is cordial?
—Persian Proverb

♦ ♦ ♦

No wonder the teacher knows so much; she has the book.
—Edgar Watson Howe

♦ ♦ ♦

Sign in window of bankrupt store: WE UNDERSOLD EVERYBODY.

♦ ♦ ♦

The guy was such a poor driver, the police gave him a season's ticket.

♦ ♦ ♦

Earl Strom, NBA referee: "Officiating is the only occupation in the world where the highest accolade is silence."

♦ ♦ ♦

Some persons never appeal to God unless they're getting licked.

♦ ♦ ♦

Silence iz one ov the hardest kind ov arguments tew refute.
—Josh Billings

Bottles and cans from the steamship Bertrand, that sank in the Missouri River 109 years ago, recently were opened and inspected. Chemists found surprisingly high levels of Vitamin C in plum tomatoes and tomato catsup. Red peppers were high in Vitamin A. The Bertrand and its cargo were discovered in 1968 under 28 feet of soil in the river bottom.

♦ ♦ ♦

Women can never be man's equal until she sports a large bald spot on the top of her head and still thinks she's handsome.

♦ ♦ ♦

The frozen-food industry began in 1925. The secret of quick-freezing was discovered by a naturalist who was ice-fishing in 20-degree-below-zero weather. A fish he caught froze almost instantly, but later revived in a pail of water, its cell structure seemingly unimpaired. Would quick-freezing keep food fresh? The naturalist thought it was worth a try. His name: Clarence Birdseye.

♦ ♦ ♦

People who are busy rowing seldom rock the boat.

♦ ♦ ♦

I'm convinced romance is here to stay. So is hot soup. With me the soup comes first.   —George Burns

♦ ♦ ♦

A bumper sticker I saw on I-80: "55 mph, it's a law we can live with," as he passed me at 65 mph.   —George Cockle

In vain we call old notions fudge,
And bend our conscience to our dealing;
The Ten Commandments will not budge,
And stealing *will* continue stealing.   —James Russell Lowell

♦ ♦ ♦

To write a love letter begin without knowing what you are going
to say and end by not knowing what you have said.

♦ ♦ ♦

It is with life as with a play—it matters not how long the action
is spun out, but how good the acting is.   —Seneca

♦ ♦ ♦

Hate or deep-seated hostility is the most inefficient use a person
can make of his mind.   —Ross L. Holman

♦ ♦ ♦

Experience keeps a dear school, yet fools will learn in no other.
          —Benjamin Franklin

♦ ♦ ♦

The road forward is uphill and hard to march. But the higher the
hill the finer the view.   —Contributed by E.H. Benner

♦ ♦ ♦

A sign on a butcher shop in London proclaims proudly: "We
make sausage for Queen Elizabeth." On a rival shop across the
street is another sign: "God save the Queen."

God gives every bird its food, but he does not throw it into the nest. —Josiah Gilbert Holland

♦ ♦ ♦

The secret of being miserable is to have the leisure to bother about whether you are happy or not. —George Bernard Shaw

♦ ♦ ♦

The surest way to make it hard for children is to make it easy for them. —Eleanor Roosevelt

♦ ♦ ♦

There is one thing to be said for ignorance—it sure causes a lot of interesting arguments.

♦ ♦ ♦

An observation made by Clarke Kerr a few years ago . . . He pointed out that the sixty-six Western institutions that have survived since the year 1530 include:
—The Roman Catholic and Lutheran Churches;
—The parliaments of Iceland and the Isle of Man; and
—Sixty-two universities. —Ronald W. Roskens

♦ ♦ ♦

If people knew how hard I have had to work to gain my mastery, it wouldn't seem wonderful at all. —Michelangelo

♦ ♦ ♦

A word fitly spoken is like apples of gold in pictures of silver. —Proverbs 25:11

166

Gravestone Epitaphs . . .

In the Boothill Museum, Dodge City, Kansas:
  Shoot-Em-Up Jake
  Run for Sheriff 1872
  Run from Sheriff 1876
  Buried 1876

Death Valley, California:
  Here lies the body of poor Aunt Charlotte
  Born a virgin, died a harlot;
  For sixteen years she kept her virginity,
  A damn'd long time for this vicinity.

On a dentist from Edinburgh, Scotland:
  Stranger, tread
  This ground with gravity;
  Dentist Brown is filling
  His last cavity.

In a small cemetery near Albany, New York:
  Harry Edsel Smith
  Born 1903—Died 1942
  Looked up the elevator shaft to see if the car was on the way down. It was.

From Burlington, Massachusetts:
  Susan Lowder
  Here lies the body of Susan Lowder
  Who burst while drinking Seidlitz powder;
  Called from this world to her heavenly rest
  She should have waited till it effervesced.

◆ ◆ ◆

That some should be rich shows that others may become rich, and hence is just encouragement to industry and enterprise. I don't believe in a law to prevent a man from getting rich; it would do more harm than good.　　　　　—Abraham Lincoln

◆ ◆ ◆

A small town is the place where a fellow with a black eye doesn't have to explain; they know.

167

The two greatest stimulants in the world are love and debt.
—Benjamin Disraeli

◆ ◆ ◆

Gutenberg's gun has the longest range!
—James Russell Lowell

◆ ◆ ◆

Love cannot stay at home; a man cannot keep it to himself. Like light, it is constantly traveling. A man must spend it, must give it away.
—Alexander MacLeod

◆ ◆ ◆

Confidence is locking a door and then not trying the knob to be sure.

◆ ◆ ◆

Have you ever stopped to think that if Adam came back today, the only thing he'd recognize would be centerfolds?
—Robert Orben

◆ ◆ ◆

Taxi driver: "Where to?"
Passenger: "Drive off a cliff—I'm committing suicide."

◆ ◆ ◆

A word of encouragement during failure is worth more than a dictionary of praise after success.

◆ ◆ ◆

When you consent, consent graciously. When you refuse, refuse firmly.

◆ ◆ ◆

When you speak to other people for their good, it is influence; and when other people speak to you for your good, it is interference.

Worry is the interest you pay today on the troubles of tomorrow.
—Dr. Clayton

♦ ♦ ♦

If you ride a horse, sit close and tight;
If you ride a man, sit easy and light.

♦ ♦ ♦

It is an approved maxim of war never to do what the enemy wishes you to do. —Napoleon I

♦ ♦ ♦

Strange to see how a good dinner and feasting reconciles everybody. —Samuel Pepys

♦ ♦ ♦

There are several good protections against temptations, but the surest is cowardice. —Mark Twain

♦ ♦ ♦

The cards you hold in the game of life mean very little—it's the way you play them that counts.

♦ ♦ ♦

It is better to know some of the questions than all of the answers. —James Thurber

♦ ♦ ♦

Old age has its pleasures, which, though different, are not less than the pleasures of youth. —W. Somerset Maugham

♦ ♦ ♦

To be able to fill leisure intelligently is the last product of civilization. —Bertrand Russell, Earl Russell

Next time you feel the surge of anger, say to yourself, "is this really worth what it's going to do to me and others emotionally? I will make a fool of myself. I may hurt someone I love, or I might lose a friend." Practice realizing that it is not worth it to get so worked up about things, and always remember Seneca, who said, "The greatest cure of anger is delay."

—Norman Vincent Peale

♦ ♦ ♦

What we customarily call a "good sermon" is one that we smugly feel applies to all the people who didn't attend services that day. —Sydney J. Harris

♦ ♦ ♦

Living without faith is like driving in a fog.

—*Hoard's Dairyman*

♦ ♦ ♦

Think small. Big ideas upset nearly everyone.

♦ ♦ ♦

You may be deceived if you trust too much, but you will live in torment if you do not trust enough. —Frank Crane

♦ ♦ ♦

Draw your wisdom from old men, and your enthusiasm from young men.

♦ ♦ ♦

Love your enemies, for they tell you your faults.

—Benjamin Franklin

♦ ♦ ♦

At times, it helps to believe in evolution and that man is not yet finished.

Make it a habit—economize on the time spent complaining.

♦ ♦ ♦

If a man could have half of his wishes, he would double his troubles. —Benjamin Franklin

♦ ♦ ♦

Many go out for wool, and come home shorn themselves.
—Miguel de Cervantes

♦ ♦ ♦

Drive-in banking was invented so cars could go in and see their real owners.

♦ ♦ ♦

What most people save for a rainy day is a request for a loan.

♦ ♦ ♦

Time often flatters the past by half erasing it.
—George Santayana

♦ ♦ ♦

There are depths in the sea which the storms that lash the surface into fury never reach. They who reach down into the depths of life where, in the stillness, the voice of God is heard, have the stabilizing power which carries them poised and serene through the hurricane of difficulties.

♦ ♦ ♦

My argument is that War makes rattling good history; but Peace is poor reading. —Thomas Hardy

♦ ♦ ♦

Anger is one letter snort of danger.

A well-developed sense of humor means a well-balanced personality. . . The better adjusted you are, the more readily you will respond to humor in jokes, cartoons, and also everyday situations. Maladjusted people show a far greater tendency to miss the point in a joke or funny remark and to take things seriously which are meant to be funny. . . . The ability to get a laugh out of everyday situations is a safety-valve ridding you of tensions which might otherwise damage your health.

♦ ♦ ♦

Really important people seldom have time to act important.

♦ ♦ ♦

The Ten Commandments contain 297 words. The Bill of Rights is stated in 463 words. Lincoln's Gettysburg Address contains 266 words. A recent Federal directive to regulate the price of cabbage contains 26,911 words. —*Atlanta Journal*

♦ ♦ ♦

A man's worth should be judged by what he does when he needn't do anything.

♦ ♦ ♦

We often wonder how the husbands of secretaries get along with *their* secretaries.

♦ ♦ ♦

The only people who can raise money easily are those who don't need it badly.

♦ ♦ ♦

One way to restore humility is to read the help-wanted ads. You'd be surprised how many positions there are which you are too ignorant, too unattractive, or too old to fill.

—*Kiwanis Magazine*

172

The violin evolved out of the lyre in the 16th century, chiefly at Brescia. Andrea Amati brought the art of violin making to Cremona and there his grandson Nicolo surpassed all rivals in the craft until he himself was excelled by his pupils Andrea Guarneri and Antonio Stradivari. These three families perfected the violin during the 16th, 17th, and 18th centuries.

The Guarneri were a dynasty; Andrea and his sons Pietro and Giuseppe I, his grandson Pietro II, and his grandnephew Giuseppe II—who made the violin preferred by Paganini to all others.

The oldest violin signed by Stradivari is dated 1666, when he was twenty-two years old. It was labeled Antonius Stradivarius Cremonensis Alumnus Nicoli Amati Faciebat Anno 1666 followed by his personal symbol—a Maltese cross and his initials, A.S., enclosed in a double circle. Later he signed himself, with proud simplicity, "Stradivarius." He worked incessantly, ate frugally and lived to ninety-three years. He amassed a fortune by the superior beauty, construction, tone, and finish of his instruments. Improving upon his instruments has proved impossible. He is known to have made 1,116 violins, violas, and violoncellos. Today 540 of his violins exist and some have sold for ten thousand dollars. The secret of his varnish has been lost. Of his eleven children, only two followed in his footsteps.

♦ ♦ ♦

Wise men, though all laws were abolished, would lead the same lives.   —Aristophanes

♦ ♦ ♦

I like two kinds of men—domestic and foreign.   —Mae West

173

Life, if well used, is long enough. —Seneca

♦ ♦ ♦

Tears are often the telescope through which men see far into heaven. —Henry Ward Beecher

♦ ♦ ♦

He is rich enough who owes nothing. —French Proverb

♦ ♦ ♦

A man is boss of the home when he doesn't mind using the guest towels.

♦ ♦ ♦

Established writers are very often besieged by young writers seeking advice or help. A story is told of the young writer seeking advice from the aged English writer W. Somerset Maugham and said: "Mr. Maugham, I've just written a novel but I haven't been able to come up with a suitable title. You seem to have such a knack for titles, sir, *Cakes and Ale*, *The Razor's Edge*, I wonder if you would read my novel and help me."

"Don't need to read your novel," the old man said. "Are there drums in it?"

"No, it's not that sort of a story. You see, it deals with the alienation of . . ."

"Are there any bugles in it?"

"No, sir."

"Call it *No Drums, No Bugles.*" —Donald Kaul

♦ ♦ ♦

A great memory does not make a philosopher, any more than a dictionary can be called a grammar. —John Henry Newman

174

Grow old along with me[1]
The best is yet to be,
The last of life, for which the first was made.
Our times are in his hand.
Who saith, "A whole I planned,
Youth shows but half; trust God: see all, nor be afraid!"
—Robert Browning

♦ ♦ ♦

Poetry teaches the enormous force of a few words, and, in proportion to the inspiration, checks loquacity.
—Ralph Waldo Emerson

♦ ♦ ♦

The power of imagination makes us infinite.   —John Muir

♦ ♦ ♦

One doesn't have to live alone to feel lonesome.

♦ ♦ ♦

By the street of By-and-By, one arrives at the house of Never.
—Miguel de Cervantes

♦ ♦ ♦

Why is it that people in the magazine ads are always beautiful, handsome, daring, dashing, or distinguished? After all, it's us moth-eaten millions of ordinary humans who buy the products.
—David Savage

♦ ♦ ♦

To reform a man, you must begin with his grandmother.
—Victor Hugo

♦ ♦ ♦

The winds and waves are already on the side of the ablest navigators.   —Edward Gibbon

If a thing is old, it is a sign that it was fit to live. Old families, old customs, old styles survive because they are fit to survive. The guarantee of continuity is quality. Submerge the good in a flood of the new, and the good will come back to join the good which the new brings with it. Old-fashioned hospitality, old-fashioned politeness, old-fashioned honor in business had qualities of survival. These will come back. —Capt. Eddie Rickenbacker

♦ ♦ ♦

Only that traveling is good which reveals to me the value of home and enables me to enjoy it better. —Henry David Thoreau

♦ ♦ ♦

No Respect . . .

Get even by using the sharpest weapon of them all—humor. Here are some favorites:

. . . I'm not going to engage in a battle of wits with you—I never attack an unarmed man.
. . . If Moses had known you, there would have been another Commandment.
. . . You have a ready wit. Let me know when it's ready.
. . . Someday you'll go too far—and I hope you'll stay there.
. . . Don't move—I want to forget you just the way you are.
. . . Is your family happy? Or do you go home at night?
. . . It's nice hearing from you. Next time, send me a postcard.
—Henny Youngman

♦ ♦ ♦

Rare is the person who can weigh the faults of others without putting his thumb on the scales. —Byron J. Langenfeld

WINTER

Blow, blow, thou winter wind,
Thou art not so unkind
   As man's ingratitude;
Thy tooth is not so keen,
Because thou art not seen,
   Although thy breath be rude.
Heigh-ho! Sing, heigh-ho! unto the green holly,
Most friendship is feigning, most loving mere folly.
   Then heigh-ho, the holly!
   This life is most jolly.

Freeze, freeze, thou bitter sky,
That dost not bite so nigh
   As benefits forgot.
Though thou the waters warp,
Thy sting is not so sharp
   As friend remembered not.
Heigh-ho! Sing, heigh-ho! unto the green holly.
Most friendship is feigning, most loving mere folly.
   Then heigh-ho, the holly!
   This life is most jolly.   —William Shakespeare

There are two ways of being happy: We must either diminish our wants or augment our means—either may do—the result is the same and it is for each man to decide for himself and to do that which happens to be easier.   —Benjamin Franklin

♦ ♦ ♦

The world of books is the most remarkable creation of man. Nothing else that he builds ever lasts. Monuments fall; nations perish; civilizations grow old and die out; and, after an era of darkness new races build orders. But in the world of books are volumes that have seen this happen again and again, and yet live on, still young, still as fresh as the day they were written, still telling men's hearts of the hearts of men centuries dead.
                    —Clarence Day

♦ ♦ ♦

2520 Mystery . . .

In the tombs discovered under the pyramids of Giza, in Egypt, a number is displayed conspicuously, chiseled deep in the numerals of an ancient people. These numerals, interpreted into figures of this day, read:
                    2520
That mystic number—2520—is divisible by any number from one to nine, and, according to mathematicians, you can't perform that miracle with any other number.

Only uncomfortable chairs become antiques. The comfortable ones are worn out by a single generation.

◆ ◆ ◆

Judge: Sam, do you swear to tell the truth, the whole truth, and nothing but the truth?
Sam: I do, Judge.
Judge: Now, Sam, what have you to say for yourself?
Sam: Judge, you have set up too many limitations.

◆ ◆ ◆

No one could tell me where my soul might be;
I searched for God, and He eluded me;
I sought my brother out, and found all three.　　—Ernest Crosby

◆ ◆ ◆

When Leonardo da Vinci was working on his painting "The Last Supper," he became angry with a certain man. Losing his temper he lashed the other fellow with bitter words and threats. Returning to his canvas he attempted to work on the face of Jesus, but was unable to do so. He was so upset he could not compose himself for the painstaking work. Finally he put down his tools and sought out the man and asked his forgiveness. He returned to his workshop and finished painting the face of Jesus.

180

FRANKLIN'S 13 SUBJECTS

1. Temperance—Eat not to dullness; drink not to elevation.

2. Silence—Speak not but what may benefit others or yourself; avoid trifling conversation.

3. Order—Let all your things have their places; let each part of your business have its time.

4. Resolution—Resolve to perform what you ought; perform without fail what you resolve.

5. Frugality—Make no expense but to do good to others or yourself; i. e., waste nothing.

6. Industry—Lose no time; be always employed in something useful; cut off all unnecessary actions.

7. Sincerity—Use no hurtful deceit; think innocently and justly, and if you speak, speak accordingly.

8. Justice—Wrong none by doing injuries, or omitting the benefits that are your duty.

9. Moderation—Avoid extremes; forbear resenting injuries so much as you think they deserve.

10. Cleanliness—Tolerate no uncleanliness in body, clothes, or habitation.

11. Tranquility—Be not disturbed at trifles, or at accidents common or unavoidable.

12. Chastity—Rarely use venery but for health or offspring, never to dullness, weakness, or the injury of your own or another's peace or reputation.

13. Humility—Imitate Jesus and Socrates.

♦ ♦ ♦

Let us consider the fascinating case of a 12-year-old who had his first date with a girl the other evening.

He was tearing around the house, getting set for the great event, when his mother reminded him he hadn't taken his bath.

"Bath?" he howled, outraged. "I got no time for a bath! I've just got 5 minutes, and you have to teach me to dance!"

♦ ♦ ♦

Let us impart all the blessings we possess, or ask for ourselves, to the whole family of mankind.　　　—George Washington

181

Why is it no one wants to own a "white elephant" and how has the term come to mean a possession that is costly to maintain and yet yields no profit?

It probably started with the fact that an actual albino elephant—even a pale gray or yellowish one—is rare, and hence was venerated in olden times in India, Ceylon, Siam, and Burma. In old Siam, for example, only the king was deemed worthy to own a white elephant. Any common man who discovered a white elephant was duty bound to put it in a special stable, hire attendants to wait on it, and never, never put it to work. Thus the term came to mean something of high upkeep, and no return.

♦ ♦ ♦

Benjamin Franklin was the youngest son of a youngest son of a youngest son of a youngest son. He was the first American philosopher. He was the first American ambassador. He invented the harmonica. He invented the rocking chair. He invented the street lamp. He was the first political cartoonist. He was the best swimmer of his time. He originated the first circulating library. He discovered the Gulf Stream. He is the originator of Daylight Savings Time. He is the father of modern dentistry. He organized the first fire department. He originated the first street-cleaning department. He invented the lightning conductor. He established the modern post-office system. He was the founder of the Democratic party. And, lastly, he was a printer!

♦ ♦ ♦

"She is a woman who has suffered a great deal for her belief," announced Mabel.

"Indeed? What is her belief?" questioned an admirer.

"She believes she can wear a No. 4 shoe on a No. 6 foot."

182

Russett and white and gray is the oak wood in the great snow.
Still from the North it comes,
Whispering, settling, sifting through the trees,
    O'erloading branch and twig
    The road is lost.
Clearing and meadow, stream and ice-bound pond are made once
    more a trackless wilderness
In the white bush where not a creature stirs;
And the pale sun is blotted from the sky.
In that strange twilight the lone traveler halts
To listen while the stealthy snowflakes fall.   —Bliss Carman

♦ ♦ ♦

Who has deceived thee so oft as thyself?
                                      —Benjamin Franklin

♦ ♦ ♦

The best laid schemes o' Mice an' Men,
    Gang aft agley,
An' lea'e us nought but grief an' pain.
    For promis'd joy!   —Robert Burns

♦ ♦ ♦

"Your methods of cultivation are hopelessly out of date," said
the youthful agricultural college graduate to the old farmer.
"Why, I'd be astonished if you got even ten pounds of apples from
that tree."
    "So would I," replied the farmer. "It's a pear tree."

♦ ♦ ♦

Keep the golden mean between saying too much and too little.
                                      —Publilius Syrus

183

Benjamin Franklin, a worldly-wise American who spent eighteen years of his life in London was close to many Britishers, wrote one of them in 1775, after the battles of Lexington, Concord, and Bunker Hill:

Mr. Strahan,

You are a member of Parliament and one of the Majority which has doomed my Country to Destruction. You have begun to burn our Towns and murder our People. Look upon your hands. They are stained with the blood of your Relations. You and I were long Friends. You are now my Enemy,

and

    I am

      Yours,

        Benjamin Franklin

Don't marry a girl because she looks sensible, because a sensible girl has more sense than to look sensible.

♦ ♦ ♦

One pound of learning requires ten pounds of common sense to apply it.   —Persian Proverb

♦ ♦ ♦

It is not permitted to the most equitable of men to be a judge in his own cause.   —Blaise Pascal

♦ ♦ ♦

There's a line on the ocean whereby crossing you can lose a day. There's one on the highway where you can do even better.

Washington was not our first president. He was the first president of the United States under the Constitution, but not the first of the nation. John Hanson, of Maryland, was the country's first under the Articles of Confederation.

Delegates in Congress from the 13 original colonies elected Hanson president November 5, 1781. 　　　　—Gloria Pitzer

♦ ♦ ♦

I have more trouble with D.L. Moody than any other man I know. 　　　　　　　　　　　　　　　—D.L. Moody

♦ ♦ ♦

I want you guys to tell me candidly what's wrong with our operation—even if it means losing your job. 　　—Sam Goldwyn

♦ ♦ ♦

If I'd known I was gonna live this long, I woulda taken better care of myself! 　　　　　　　　　　　—Jimmy Durante

♦ ♦ ♦

Don't tell other people your troubles. Half of them aren't interested and the other half are glad you got what you had coming to you.

♦ ♦ ♦

I have often regretted my speech, never my silence.
　　　　　　　　　　　　　　　　—Publilius Syrus

Church bulletins sometimes should never have seen the light of day. The reason why is evident in this collection of church bulletin announcements sent to us by the Rev. Stanley H. Conover of St. Louis Park, Minnesota. He came across the collection, uncredited to any source, in a local nursing home newsletter. So we can't vouch that everything was misannounced as shown. But does it matter?

"This afternoon there will be a meeting in the South and North ends of the Church. Children will be baptized at both ends."

"The Service will close with 'Little Drops of Water.' One of the ladies will start quietly and the rest of the congregation will join in."

"On Sunday, a special collection will be taken to defray the expenses of the new carpet. All those wishing to do something on the carpet please come forward and get a piece of paper."

"The ladies of the church have cast off clothing of every kind, and they may be seen in the church basement on Friday afternoon."

"Thursday at 5:00 p.m. there will be a meeting of the Little Mothers Club. All wishing to become little mothers will please meet the minister in his study."

"Wednesday, the Ladies Literary Society will meet. Mrs. Johnson will sing 'Put Me in My Little Bed,' accompanied by the preacher."

◆ ◆ ◆

The bathtub was invented in 1850 and the phone in 1875. In 1850, you could've sat in the tub without having the phone ring.

◆ ◆ ◆

After the family moved into a larger house, their six-year-old was asked how he liked his new home.
"It's just great," he said, "I have my own room, and so do my sisters. But poor mom is still in with dad."

◆ ◆ ◆

Heredity is what makes parents of teenagers wonder about each other.

Many cities and states have cooked up some pretty unusual laws when it comes to food. Here's an interesting helping of just a few. It is illegal to:

Take a streetcar or go to a theater within four hours of consuming garlic (Gary, Indiana).

Munch on peanuts in church or use tomatoes in clam chowder (Massachusetts).

Sell milk by the glass (San Francisco, California).

Sell pickles that fall apart when dropped 12 inches (Connecticut).

Drink coffee after 6 P.M., if you're a young woman (Corvalis, Oregon).

Sell beer, if you're a tavern operator, unless you're simultaneously cooking soup (Nebraska).

Use a broom to sweep floors if you're a restaurant operator (Birmingham, Alabama).

Sell rye bread, goose liver, or limburger cheese on Sunday (Houston, Texas).

♦ ♦ ♦

Nothing's better for baldness than being a baby.

♦ ♦ ♦

If you want the time to pass quickly just give your note for 90 days.   *—Farmers Almanac,* 1797

♦ ♦ ♦

There is no dignity quite so impressive, and no independence quite so important, as living within your means.

—Calvin Coolidge

♦ ♦ ♦

Far too many of us listen to a new idea with our prejudices.

187

Space—Black Holes . . .

American astronomers think they have pinpointed at least two black holes out in the heavens. Russians theorize there may be billions of them. In any event, if the existence of even one can be proved, it stands to reason there could be more. One rather far out idea, in more ways than one, is that the powerful black holes may be open-ended, something like a tornado funnel and spewing colossal amounts of matter and energy into remote areas of the universe—or even into other universes and time.

♦ ♦ ♦

Conscience gets a lot of credit that belongs to cold feet.

♦ ♦ ♦

While money isn't everything, it does help you to find that out in comfort.

♦ ♦ ♦

I would uphold the law if for no other reason but to protect myself.   —Sir Thomas More

♦ ♦ ♦

Boy to his mother: "You never mention the dirt I track out!"

♦ ♦ ♦

The actor pleaded with the agent to at least see his act. "My act is different. Look—I fly." Then he lifted his arms and flew around the room and landed on the desk.

"Okay," said the agent. "So you can imitate birds. What else can you do?"

♦ ♦ ♦

Did you ever notice that the networks never interrupt commercials with "This special bulletin just in . . ."?

Cut your own wood and it will warm you twice.
—Old Chinese Proverb

♦ ♦ ♦

If a little knowledge is dangerous, where is the man who has so much as to be out of danger? —T.H. Huxley

♦ ♦ ♦

Many a man has fallen in love with a girl in a light so dim he would not have chosen a suit by it. —Maurice Chevalier

♦ ♦ ♦

Learning makes a man fit company for himself.
—Edward Young

♦ ♦ ♦

We are shaped and fashioned by what we love. —Goethe

♦ ♦ ♦

A vein of poetry exists in the hearts of all men.
—Thomas Carlyle

♦ ♦ ♦

One of the best rules in conversation is, never to say a thing which any of the company can reasonably wish had been left unsaid. —Jonathan Swift

♦ ♦ ♦

Alexander the Great had a famous horse, Bucephalus. No one could ride him except Alexander. Bucephalus was afraid of his shadow. Solution: Alexander rode towards the sun. If you always face the Light, the shadows of failure and illness fall behind you.
—*Phoenix Flame*

What can be more palpably absurd and ridiculous than the prospect held out of locomotives traveling twice as fast as stage coaches? We should as soon expect the people of Woolrich to suffer themselves to be fired off on one of Congreve's richochet rockets as trust themselves to the mercy of a machine going at such a rate. We will back old Father Thames against the Woolrich Railways for any sum. We trust that Parliament will, in all railways it may sanction, limit the speed to eight or nine miles an hour, which we entirely agree with Mr. Sylvester "is as great as can be ventured with safety."   —*Quarterly Review,* 1825

◆ ◆ ◆

Education is not given for the purpose of earning a living; it's learning what to do with a living after you earn it.
—Abraham Lincoln

◆ ◆ ◆

Keep on going and the chances are that you will stumble on something, perhaps when you are least expecting it. I have never heard of anyone stumbling on something sitting down.
—Charles F. Kettering

◆ ◆ ◆

It was a Christmas turkey of truly Herculean proportions. Seated around the table, the guests gazed with mouth-watering anticipation as the maid bore it into the dining room. Halfway between the door and the table lay a tiny marble Johnnie had carelessly left there. The maid stepped on it, and fell flat on her face while the big turkey scooted across the floor.

But the hostess was a woman of miraculous resource.

"Don't worry, Mary," she counseled calmly. "Just take it back to the kitchen and bring in the other one."

190

Requiem . . .

Under the wide and starry sky
Dig the grave and let me lie.
Glad did I live and gladly die,
And I laid me down with a will.

This be the verse you grave for me:
Here he lies where he longed to be;
Home is the sailor, home from the sea,
And the hunter home from the hill.   —Robert Louis Stevenson

♦ ♦ ♦

Hate is like acid. It can damage the vessel in which it is stored as
well as destroy the object on which it is poured.   —Ann Landers

♦ ♦ ♦

On the photo department door at the *Jackson Daily News* in
Mississippi is the sign: "Please keep darkroom door closed. If it is
left open, all the dark leaks out."

♦ ♦ ♦

There is only one thing people like that is good for them; a good
night's sleep.   —Edgar Watson Howe

♦ ♦ ♦

Celery has negative calories—it takes more calories to eat a
piece of celery than the celery has in it to begin with.

♦ ♦ ♦

A flashlight is what you carry dead batteries in.

♦ ♦ ♦

Why didn't Noah just swat both flies?

A Third Grader's Essay on:
What a Grandmother is . . .

A grandmother is a lady who has no children of her own, so she likes other people's little girls and boys. A grandfather is a man grandmother. He goes for walks with the boys and they talk about fishing and tractors and like that.

Grandmas don't have to do anything except be there. They're old, so they shouldn't play hard or run. It is enough if they drive us to the market where the pretend horse is, and have lots of dimes ready. Or, if they take us for walks, they should slow down past things like pretty leaves and caterpillars. They should never say "hurry up."

Usually they are fat, but not too fat to tie kids' shoes. They wear glasses and funny underwear. They can take their teeth and gums off.

It is better if they don't typewrite or play cards except with us. They don't have to be smart, only answer questions like why dogs hate cats, and how come God isn't married. They don't talk baby talk like visitors do, because it is hard to understand. When they read to us, they don't skip or mind if it is the same story again. Everybody should try to have one, especially if you don't have television, because grandmas are the only grown-ups who have got time.

♦ ♦ ♦

Never run after your own hat—others will be delighted to do it; why spoil their fun?   —Mark Twain

♦ ♦ ♦

Movies will reach a new high in realism when the detective following a suspect can't find a place to park his car.

If thou of fortune be bereft,
And in thy store there be but left
Two loaves—sell one, and with the dole
Buy hyacinths to feed they soul.   —James Terry White

♦ ♦ ♦

If we wish to appreciate him, [Lincoln] we have only to conceive the inevitable chaos in which we should now be weltering, had a weak man or an unwise one been chosen in his stead.
—James Russell Lowell

♦ ♦ ♦

Three may keep a secret, if two of them are dead.
—Benjamin Franklin

♦ ♦ ♦

Early in his career Winston Churchill sported a mustache. At a dinner party Churchill was holding forth with vigor on politics, when a young woman near him said, "I dislike both your politics and your mustache." "Don't distress yourself, my dear lady," said Churchill. "You are unlikely to come into contact with either."

♦ ♦ ♦

Happiness is only a by-product of successful living.
—Dr. Austen Fox Riggs

♦ ♦ ♦

It's hard to get up early in the morning when you're wearing silk pajamas.   —Eddie Arcaro

♦ ♦ ♦

One advantage of letting your conscience be your guide is you won't run into any heavy traffic.

Politics are almost as exciting as war, and quite as dangerous. In war you can only be killed once, but in politics many times.

—Winston Churchill

♦ ♦ ♦

Many great ideas have been lost because the people who had them couldn't stand being laughed at.

♦ ♦ ♦

Life is a magic vase filled to the brim; so that you cannot dip into it nor draw from it; but it overflows into the hand that drops treasures into it—drop in malice and it overflows hate; drop in charity and it overflows love.

—John Ruskin

♦ ♦ ♦

The sincere alone can recognize sincerity.   —Thomas Carlyle

♦ ♦ ♦

The successful people are the ones who can look up stuff for the rest of the world to keep busy at.

—Donald Marquis

♦ ♦ ♦

Mankind are very odd creatures: one half censure what they practice, the other half practice what they censure.

—Benjamin Franklin

♦ ♦ ♦

One reason folks get into trouble is that trouble usually starts out being fun.

♦ ♦ ♦

Sign on a hen house: An egg a day keeps Colonel Sanders away.

♦ ♦ ♦

If exercise is so good for you, why do athletes have to retire at about age 35?

Stopping By Woods On A
Snowy Evening . . .

Whose woods these are I think I know.
His house is in the village though;
He will not see me stopping here
To watch his woods fill up with snow.

My little horse must think it queer
To stop without a farmhouse near
Between the woods and frozen lake
The darkest evening of the year.

He gives his harness bells a shake
To ask if there is some mistake.
The only other sound's the sweep
Of easy wind and downy flake.

The woods are lovely, dark and deep.
But I have promises to keep,
And miles to go before I sleep,
And miles to go before I sleep.   —Robert Frost

♦ ♦ ♦

The history of the world is the record of man in quest of his
daily bread and butter.   —Hendrik Willem Van Loon

♦ ♦ ♦

Who serves his country well has no need of ancestors.
                                                    —Voltaire

♦ ♦ ♦

Leisure is the time for doing something useful.
                                        —Benjamin Franklin

♦ ♦ ♦

Then there was the little boy who ran to his mother and said,
"Daddy took me to the zoo, and one of the animals paid $48.40
across the board."

BELIEVE IT OR NOT:

In 1836 Andrew Jackson not only had the U.S.A. out of debt for the first time in our history but also had a surplus of $37,468,859!! He turned over the White House to Martin Van Buren in 1837 and by 1840 we owed 21 cents per capita and have never been out of debt since.

♦ ♦ ♦

Janet: "He's always a perfect gentleman when he's with me."
Mary: "He bores me too."

♦ ♦ ♦

No one is rich enough to do without a neighbor.
—*York Trade Compositor*

♦ ♦ ♦

We must all remember that a government big enough to give us everything we want is a government big enough to take from us everything we have.　　　　　　　　　—Gerald Ford

♦ ♦ ♦

At the age of twenty, we don't care what the world thinks of us; at thirty we worry about what it is thinking of us; at forty we discover that it wasn't thinking of us at all.

♦ ♦ ♦

A perpetual holiday is a good working definition of hell.
—George Bernard Shaw

♦ ♦ ♦

The mind has real need of contact, at close intervals, with the soil.　　　　　　　　　—André Maurois

196

It might be well to bear in mind, Olin Miller reminds us, that while "billion" and "million" are similar in sound, their ratio is the same as that of a ten-dollar bill and a penny.

♦ ♦ ♦

Sweet are the uses of adversity,
Which, like the toad, ugly and venomous,
Wears yet a precious jewel on his head;
And this our life, exempt from public haunt,
Finds tongues in trees, books in the running brooks,
Sermons in stones, and good in everything.
—William Shakespeare

♦ ♦ ♦

When it comes to a choice between two evils, I always choose the one I haven't tried before.   —Mae West

♦ ♦ ♦

And makes us rather bear those ills we have
Than fly to others that we know not of?   —William Shakespeare

♦ ♦ ♦

Fortune, when she caresses a man too much, makes him a fool.
—Publilius Syrus

♦ ♦ ♦

If you want to make a dangerous man your friend, let him do you a favor.   —Lewis E. Lawes

♦ ♦ ♦

Tomatoes should only be eaten in months with a G in them.

♦ ♦ ♦

Life consists in what a man is thinking of all day.
—Ralph Waldo Emerson

♦ ♦ ♦

Man is what he believes.   —Anton Chekhov

197

An acquaintance is a person whom we know well enough to borrow from, but not well enough to lend to.   —Ambrose Bierce

♦ ♦ ♦

Advice to a man about to get married:
"Never get so busy bringing home the bacon that you forget the old applesauce."

♦ ♦ ♦

The lust of avarice has so totally seized upon mankind that their wealth seems to possess them than they possess their wealth.
—Pliny

♦ ♦ ♦

Real unselfishness consists in sharing the interests of others.
—George Santayana

♦ ♦ ♦

Never take from any man his song.

♦ ♦ ♦

I love a hand that meets my own with a grasp that causes some sensation.   —F.S. Osgood

♦ ♦ ♦

Every vacation has at least two good days of weather—the day you leave and the day you get back.

♦ ♦ ♦

For age is opportunity no less
Than youth itself, though in another dress,
And as the evening twilight fades away
The sky is filled with stars, invisible by day.
—Henry Wadsworth Longfellow

Nellie Bly was a reporter on the *New York World*, and in November 1889, undertook to make a trip around the world for her paper to demonstrate the feasibility of the adventure recorded in Jules Verne's novel, *Around the World in 80 Days.* She accomplished the trip in 72 days, 6 hours, and 11 minutes. Miss Bly used steamboats, railroad trains, and horse vehicles exclusively, this being before the era of automobiles and flying machines.

♦ ♦ ♦

1946—Already thousands of would-be travelers are enthusiastically window-shopping for a trip abroad soon after V-Day. More than 500 requests are on file at the Holland-America Line for space on the Nieuw Amsterdam's first postwar sailing. On the day Paris was liberated, the French Line's New York office received 400 requests for passage to France.

The most important factor in the prospective stampede is, of course, the airplane. Formerly thousands of Americans were barred from vacationing abroad because ships took five or more days to cross and an equal time to return, thus using up most of their holiday. After the war a stenographer will be able to leave Friday after office hours, spend two weeks shopping on the Rue de la Paix, and board a Sunday-night plane that will return her to her typewriter on Monday morning.

And rates will be so low that an American businessman will be able to take his wife and children to Europe as inexpensively as they formerly spent their two weeks' vacation in summer travel at home.   —Deena Clark

It is estimated that 300 words make up 75 percent of all the words used in common speech and writing; 1,000 words form 90 percent; 2,000 more than 95 percent; 3,000, 98 percent; 4,000, 99 percent; and 6,000, 99½ percent. Ten words form more than a fourth of all these used: the, and, to, you, of, be, in, we, have, and it. The first three of these are the words used most frequently.

◆ ◆ ◆

Beware
Of entrance to a quarrel, but, being in,
Bear 't that th' opposed may beware of thee.
Give every man thy ear, but few thy voice;
Take each man's censure, but reserve thy judgment.
Costly thy habit as thy purse can buy,
But not expressed in fancy; rich, not gaudy;
For the apparel oft proclaims the man.　　—William Shakespeare

◆ ◆ ◆

William Penn, the Quaker founder of Pennsylvania, was a slaveholder. He attempted to educate his slaves and improve their moral standards and family relations in every way possible. In his last will he provided that all the slaves owned by him should be given their freedom. The Quakers in later years were almost unanimously opposed to the institution of slavery and many of them were leaders in the abolition movement.

◆ ◆ ◆

It was a deathbed scene, but the director was not satisfied with the hero's acting.
"Come on" he cried. "Put more life into your dying."

◆ ◆ ◆

Even a fool, when he holdeth his peace, is counted wise.
　　　　　　　　　　　　　　　　　　　—Old Proverb

The old saying that many great inventions are the products of accidents seems to hold true in the culinary field.

There is a tradition surrounding the origin of Melba toast, which was supposedly a creation of the great French master chef, Escoffier. At the Savoy in London, César Ritz was maitre d'hotel and Escoffier was chef. Nellie Melba, celebrated prima donna, was staying there and was strenuously dieting, living largely on toast.

It chanced one day, while the master was preoccupied, that an underling prepared the great lady's toast. It was bungled and served to her in a thin dried-up state resembling parchment. Ritz beheld in horror his celebrated guest crunching this aborted toast, and hastened over to apologize. Before he could utter a word Madame Melba burst out joyfully, saying, "César, how clever of Escoffier. I have never eaten such lovely toast."

◆ ◆ ◆

You've gut to git up airly
Ef you want to take in God.   —James Russell Lowell

✝

◆ ◆ ◆

With the fearful strain that is on me day and night if I did not laugh, I should die.   —Abraham Lincoln

◆ ◆ ◆

A good storyteller is a person who has a good memory and hopes other people haven't.   —Irvin S. Cobb

◆ ◆ ◆

One of the two girls in the subway was glancing at a newspaper. "I see," she remarked presently to her companion, "that Mr. So and So, the octogenarian, is dead. Now, what on earth is an octogenarian anyhow?" "I'm sure I haven't the slightest idea," the other girl replied. "But they're an awful sickly lot. You never hear of one but he's dying."

201

One day in the Yosemite Valley, a traveler was told that there was an old man in the office of the hotel who in 1851 had been one of the company that had discovered the Yosemite. Eagerly he seized the opportunity of finding out what it was like to be the first of civilized men to behold one of nature's most marvelous works. "It must have been wonderful," he said, "to have the Valley burst suddenly upon you."

The old man spat over the edge of the veranda and looked reflective for a moment. "Well," he said, "I'll tell ye. If I'd ha' knowed it was going to be so famous I'd ha' looked at it."

♦ ♦ ♦

The way to look ahead is to look back. When you take a squint along the gun barrel of the past, you don't feel so bad about the future.   —Homer Croy

♦ ♦ ♦

The U.S.S. Constitution, "Old Ironsides," as a combat vessel carried 48,600 gallons of fresh water for a crew of 475. This was sufficient to last through six months at sea. Total evaporators installed—none. On August 23, 1779, the Constitution set sail from Boston. She carried 474 officers and men, 48,600 gallons of fresh water, 7,400 cannon shots, 11,600 pounds of black powder, and 7,000 gallons of rum. Permission to harass and destroy English shipping was given. Making Jamaica on October 6, she took on 620 pounds of flour and 68,300 gallons of rum. Then she headed for the Azores, arriving there on November 15. She provisioned with 500 pounds of beef and 4,300 gallons of Portuguese wine. On November 18, she set sail for England. In the ensuing days, she defeated five British men-of-war and captured and scuttled 12 English merchant ships, salvaging only the rum. By January 27, her powder and shot were exhausted. Unarmed she made a night raid at the Firth of Clyde. The landing party captured a whiskey distillery and transferred 40,000 gallons aboard by dawn. Then she headed home. The U.S.S. Constitution arrived in Boston in February, 1780, with no cannon shots, no powder, no food, no rum, no whiskey, no wine and 48,000 gallons of stagnant water.   —Leo Aikmann
Atlanta Constitution

♦ ♦ ♦

Be a life long or short, its completeness depends on what it was lived for.   —David Starr Jordan

202

While Benjamin Franklin was on his way from France to America in 1785, when he was seventy-nine years old, he stopped a few days at an inn in Southampton, England. In his diary he kept at the time he says: "I went at noon to bathe in Martin's salt-water hot-bath, and, floating on my back, fell asleep, and slept near an hour by my watch, without sinking or turning over! A thing I never did before, and should hardly have thought possible. Water is the easiest bed that can be." Franklin in his youth prided himself on being a good swimmer, and in his Autobiography tells us that during his first stay in England he once performed "many feats of activity, both upon and under the water" of the Thames between Chelsea and Blackfriar's. He taught two lads to be good swimmers "at twice going into the water," and at one time he seriously considered opening a swimming-school as a means of livelihood.

◆ ◆ ◆

I have so many evidences of God's direction that I cannot doubt this power comes from above. I am satisfied that when the Almighty wants me to do or not to do any particular thing, He finds a way of letting me know it.   —Abraham Lincoln

◆ ◆ ◆

The editor of the country paper went home to supper, smiling radiantly.

"Have you had some good luck?" his wife questioned.

"Luck! I should say so. Deacon Tracey, who hasn't paid his subscription for ten years, came in and stopped his paper."

◆ ◆ ◆

A farmer visited his son's college.

Watching students in a chemistry class, he was told they were looking for a universal solvent.

"What's that?" asked the farmer.

"A liquid that will dissolve anything."

"That's a great idea," agreed the farmer. "When you find it, what are you going to keep it in?"

By night an atheist half believes in God.

♦ ♦ ♦

There are more old drunkards than old doctors.

—Benjamin Franklin

♦ ♦ ♦

It is easier to fight for one's principles than to live up to them.

—Alfred Adler

♦ ♦ ♦

A lie travels around the world while truth is putting on its boots.

—Spurgeon

♦ ♦ ♦

There are only a handful of things a man likes, generation to generation.

—Archibald MacLeish

♦ ♦ ♦

Say not you know another entirely, till you have divided an inheritance with him.

—Johann Kaspar Lavater

♦ ♦ ♦

The probability that we may fail in the struggle ought not to deter us from the support of a cause we believe to be just.

—Abraham Lincoln

♦ ♦ ♦

A small boy had been vaccinated. The doctor prepared to bandage his sore arm.

"Put it on the other arm, Doctor," the boy said.

"Why," said the physician. "I want to put the bandage on your sore arm so it won't get hurt."

"Put it on the other arm, Doc," the boy insisted. "You don't know the fellows at our school."

Did you ever stop to wonder who invented the old-fashioned stove—or bifocal glasses—who first advocated the use of copper for roofs—who conceived of a damper for chimneys—who first pointed out that white is the coolest thing to wear in summer—who invented the long pole that is now used in grocery stores to reach articles on top shelves—who thought of a combined chair and stepladder—who was responsible for the paving and lighting of streets—who thought it would be nice to have trees bordering both sides of streets—who formed the first library company—first fire company—the first American fire insurance company—who founded the dead letter office and the penny post—who was responsible for American university education? Well, it was Benjamin Franklin, who incidentally was the first president of America's oldest university—the University of Pennsylvania.

♦ ♦ ♦

Visitor: "And what will you do, little girl, when you get as big as your mother?"
Little Girl: "Diet!"

♦ ♦ ♦

The housemaid was complaining to another that her mistress was demanding so much of her at large dinner parties, even insisting that all dinner plates be warmed.
"My lady used to insist on it too," said the other, "but now I just warm her plate, and everything is O.K."

♦ ♦ ♦

Nicholas I of Russia had asked Liszt, the great pianist, to play at court. Right in the middle of the opening number, the great musician looked at the Czar and saw him talking to an aide. He continued playing, but was very much irritated. As the Czar did not stop, Liszt finally quit playing. The Czar sent a messenger to ask why he was not playing and Liszt said: "When the Czar speaks everyone should be silent." Thereafter there was no interruption in the concert.

205

No one knows what music is. It is performed, listened to, composed, and talked about; but its essential reality is as little understood as that of its first cousin, electricity. We know that it detaches the understanding, enabling thoughts to turn inward upon themselves and clarify; we know that it releases the human spirit into some solitude of meditation where the creative process can freely act; we know that it can soothe pain, relieve anxiety, comfort distress, exhilarate health, confirm courage, inspire clear and bold thinking, ennoble the will, refine taste, uplift the heart, stimulate intellect, and do many another interesting and beautiful thing. And yet, when all is said and done, no one knows what music is. Perhaps the explanation is that music is the very stuff of creation itself. —Lucien Price

♦ ♦ ♦

Adversity introduces a man to himself.

♦ ♦ ♦

Anger blows out the lamp of the mind. In the explanation of a great and important question, every one should be serene, slow-pulsed, and calm. —Ingersoll

♦ ♦ ♦

Never argue at the dinner table for the one who is not hungry always gets the best of the argument.

♦ ♦ ♦

Doctor: "What was the most you ever weighed?"
Patient: "154 pounds."
Doctor: "And what was the least you ever weighed?"
Patient: "8 ¼ pounds."

206

As he was drilling a batch of recruits the sergeant saw that one of them was marching out of step. Going to the man as they marched, he said sarcastically:

"Do you know they are all out of step except you?"

"What?" asked the recruit innocently.

"I said they are all out of step except you," repeated the sergeant.

"Well," was the retort, "you tell 'em. You're in charge."

♦ ♦ ♦

"Mother, I'm the best-looking boy in Sunday School."

"Why, Tommy, who told you that?"

"Nobody, Mother, nobody didn't have to tell me. I saw the rest of them."

♦ ♦ ♦

The common wasp which makes big, ball-like nests in the trees was the first papermaker. For hundreds of years men have experimented in making paper, using various materials but have come back, for most paper requirements, to the very same material the wasp uses—wood pulp.

The first men to make paper were the Chinese—it was so many years ago that historians cannot set a definite date.

Arabs and Moors plundering Chinese Turkestan brought back captives, some of whom were papermakers and, as the Moslem law provided that they might win their freedom by working at their trade, papermaking became known outside of China.

Then the Crusaders came marching and the secrets of papermaking moved farther west. Paper mills were established in Spain, Italy, France, Switzerland, Holland—and finally in England.

It was not until 1690 that the first paper mill was established in America, near Philadelphia. Today in this country statistics show that the average citizen uses, in one way or another, over 226 pounds of paper per year. This totals twice as much poundage as the meat he consumes and indicates the giant proportions to which the paper industry has grown.

Joe: "Do you think it's possible for any woman to keep a secret?"

Charley: "Sure—my wife and I decided to get the new car several weeks before she told me about it."

♦ ♦ ♦

Anyone can become angry—that is easy; but to be angry with the right person, and to the right degree, and at the right time, and for the right purpose, and in the right way—that is not within everybody's power, and is not easy.   —Aristotle

♦ ♦ ♦

Once upon a time, they say, a man who invented a mousetrap believed his fortune would be made if he could get President Lincoln to recommend it. After a long, persistent effort, he was given audience with the President, and received the following "recommendation":

"For the sort of people who want this sort of thing this is the sort of thing that that sort of people will want."

♦ ♦ ♦

We think our civilization near its meridian, but we are yet only at the cock-crowing and the morning star.

—Ralph Waldo Emerson

♦ ♦ ♦

A pig bought on credit is forever grunting   —Spanish Proverb

Voltaire said that in 100 years the Bible would be a forgotten book, found only in the museums. When the 100 years were up, Voltaire's home was occupied by the Geneva Bible Society.
—*Sunshine Magazine*

♦ ♦ ♦

I trust a good deal to common fame, as we all must. If a man has good corn, or wood, or boards, or pigs, to sell, or can make better chairs or knives, crucibles or church organs, than anybody else, you will find a broad, hard-beaten road to his house, though it be in the woods.
—Ralph Waldo Emerson

♦ ♦ ♦

A customer sat down at a table in a smart restaurant and tied a napkin around his neck. The manager called the waiter and said to him, "Try to make that man understand as tactfully as possible that that's not done here."

The waiter approached the customer and said, "Shave or a haircut, sir?"

♦ ♦ ♦

When you are hungry spend your last dollar the day after.
—Greek Proverb

♦ ♦ ♦

What a bore it is, waking up in the morning always the same person. —Logan Pearsall Smith

♦ ♦ ♦

Man became free when he recognized that he was subject to law. —Will Durant

♦ ♦ ♦

The man who is ungrateful is often less to blame than his benefactor. —La Rochefoucauld

Roland Diller, who was one of Lincoln's neighbors in Springfield, tells the following story:

"I was called to the door one day by the cries of children in the street, and there was Mr. Lincoln, striding by with two of the boys, both of whom were wailing aloud. 'Why, Mr. Lincoln, what's the matter with the boys?' I asked. 'Just what's the matter with the whole world,' Lincoln replied, 'I've got three walnuts, and each wants two.'"

♦ ♦ ♦

See only that you work and you cannot escape the reward.
— Ralph Waldo Emerson

♦ ♦ ♦

Science gives us knowledge but only philosophy can give wisdom.
— Will Durant

♦ ♦ ♦

Blessed is the man who, having nothing to say, abstains from giving wordy evidence of the fact.
— George Eliot

♦ ♦ ♦

The Bank of England is not a government institution, but the largest private banking house in the world, with the British Government as its chief customer. It does a regular banking business and is controlled by a governor, deputy-governor and twenty-four directors. The bank was opened for business January 1, 1695.

♦ ♦ ♦

Truth, crushed to earth, shall rise again—
    The eternal years of God are hers;
But Error, wounded, writhes in pain,
    And dies among his worshipers.
— William Cullen Bryant

Friendly Old Soul: "What's the matter, little boy? Haven't you anybody to play with?"
Little Boy: "Yes, I have one friend—but I hate him."

♦ ♦ ♦

Susie: "Mamma, you know that vase you said had been handed down from generation to generation?"
Mother: "Yes, my dear."
Susie: "Well, this generation has just dropped it."

♦ ♦ ♦

Yale and Harvard had broken off athletic relations for years, but finally arrangements were made that they should compete with each other again. As the officials were about to leave after the conference, the Yale coach said, "Well, may the best team win." The Harvard coach quickly replied, "You mean may the better team win."

♦ ♦ ♦

Seat belts may be uncomfortable, but have you ever tried a stretcher?

♦ ♦ ♦

A little philosophy inclineth man's mind to atheism, but depth in philosophy bringeth men's minds about to religion.
—Francis Bacon

♦ ♦ ♦

Six evils must be overcome in this world by a man who desires prosperity: sleep, sloth, fear, anger, idleness, and procrastination.
—Hindu Proverb

♦ ♦ ♦

Pay what you owe, and you'll know what is your own.
—Benjamin Franklin

Thomas Jefferson wrote this epitaph to be placed on his tombstone after his death: "Here lies Thomas Jefferson, author of the Declaration of Independence, of the Statute for Religious Freedom in Virginia, and founder of the University of Virginia." The epitaph is particularly interesting in that Jefferson did not see fit to mention in it the Presidency of the United States.

♦ ♦ ♦

A trial in a court of justice is a trial of many things besides the prisoner at the bar. It is a trial of the strength of the laws, of the power of the Government, of the duty of the citizens, of the fidelity to conscience, and the intelligence of the jury. It is a trial of those great principles of faith, of duty, of law, of civil society, that distinguish the condition of civilization from that of barbarism.   —William Maxwell Evarts

♦ ♦ ♦

Remember that old saying—if life hands you a lemon, squeeze it and start a lemonade stand.
                —Robert E. Williams

♦ ♦ ♦

To know is nothing at all; to imagine is everything.
                                                —Anatole France

♦ ♦ ♦

What is there illustrious that is not attended by labor?
                                                —Cicero

♦ ♦ ♦

"Tommy, what is a synonym?" the teacher asked.
"A synonym," said Tommy, wisely, "is a word you use when you can't spell the other one."

212

"The world is too much with us . . ."

The world is too much with us; late and soon,
Getting and spending, we lay waste our powers:
Little we see in nature that is ours;
We have given our hearts away, a sordid boon!
This Sea that bares her bosom to the moon;
The Winds that will be howling at all hours
And are up-gathered now like sleeping flowers;
For this, for every thing, we are out of tune;
It moves us not—Great God! I'd rather be
A Pagan suckled in a creed outworn;
So might I, standing on this pleasant lea,
Have glimpses that would make me less forlorn;
Have sight of Proteus coming from the sea;
Or hear old Triton blow his wreathed horn.
                                    —William Wordsworth

♦ ♦ ♦

People get tired of everything, and of nothing sooner than of
what they most like.   —George Bernard Shaw

♦ ♦ ♦

A rich man spent a lot of money on underwater scuba equipment. He bought the works and tried out all the parts.

While deep underwater, he saw a man who had no equipment.
He couldn't understand it. So he took out his special underwater
writing set and he wrote a message asking how the man did it
without any gear.

The man grabbed the pen and wrote back: "You idiot! I'm
drowning!"

♦ ♦ ♦

You can't help a man uphill without getting closer to the top
yourself.

213

Abraham Lincoln failed in business in 1831. He was defeated for the Illinois State Legislature in 1833. His sweetheart died in 1835, and he had a nervous breakdown in 1836. He was defeated for Congress in 1843 and, after being elected in 1846, lost his Congressional seat in 1848.

He was defeated for the Senate in 1855, lost out for the vice president in 1856 and was defeated again for the Senate in 1858.

Today, there is a memorial in Washington to this great President.

♦ ♦ ♦

Perfect love sometimes does not come till the first grandchild.
—Welsh Proverb

♦ ♦ ♦

Proverbs are in the world of thought what gold coin is in the world of business—great value in small compass, and equally current among all people. Sometimes the proverb may be false, the coin counterfeit, but in both cases the false proves the value of the true.
—D. March

♦ ♦ ♦

The great man is he who does not lose his child's heart.
—Mencius

♦ ♦ ♦

I was lucky in my career, by and large. I had to work hard, but I enjoy working hard. I don't think that's a penalty at all. Most people are not allowed to work hard in the thing they like to do. And the profession I'm in is fun.
—Katharine Hepburn

Doctor (to patient): "Look at it this way. You're in excellent shape for a man of sixty-five. Forget the fact that you're only forty-five."

♦ ♦ ♦

A woman whose recently deceased husband failed to leave any insurance was asked where she got her new diamond ring. She replied, "Well, he left $1,000 for his casket and $5,000 for a stone. This is the stone."

♦ ♦ ♦

Having served on various committees, I have drawn up a list of rules: Never arrive on time; this stamps you as a beginner. Don't say anything until the meeting is half over; this stamps you as being wise. Be as vague as possible; this avoids irritating others. When in doubt, suggest that a subcommittee be appointed. Be first to move for adjournment; this will make you popular; it's what everyone is waiting for.   —Harry Chapman

♦ ♦ ♦

Can you imagine today's children 40 years from now on a psychoanalyst's couch trying to remember what they had to do without?

♦ ♦ ♦

The most difficult thing in the world to know is how to do something and to watch somebody else doing it wrong, without comment.   —Theodore H. White

♦ ♦ ♦

No one should make such thorough preparation for the rainy days that he can't enjoy today's sunshine.

♦ ♦ ♦

Money won't buy friendship but a good set of jumper cables will.

An office boy noticed two women with the boss and asked, "Who were those two girls?"

Boss: "Well, one was my wife and the other was Marilyn Monroe."

Office boy: "Which one was Marilyn Monroe?"

The boss took a dollar out of his pocket and gave it to the boy.

Office boy: "What's this for?"

Boss: "Nothing. I just want you to remember when you get to be president that I once loaned you money."

♦ ♦ ♦

A foreman caught one of his men with his eyes closed, but he had to admit the fellow's excuse was a new one. "What's the matter," the man wanted to know, "can't a guy say a prayer once in a while?"

♦ ♦ ♦

A clergyman, famous for his collection abilities, was speaking to a group of Sunday school children. When comparing himself—the pastor of a church—to a shepherd, and his congregation to the sheep, he put the following question to the children: "What does the shepherd do for the sheep?"

To the amusement of those present, a little fellow in the front row answered, "Shears them!"

♦ ♦ ♦

Work is devout, and service is divine.
Who stoops to scrub a floor
May worship more
Than he who kneels before a holy shrine;
Who crushes stubborn ore
More worthily adore
Than he who crushes sacramental wine.

—Roy Campbell MacFie

216

Nothing makes you a better listener than hearing your name mentioned.

♦ ♦ ♦

No one is exempt from talking nonsense; the mistake is to do it solemnly.   —Montaigne

♦ ♦ ♦

A group of mothers and children were waiting for the pediatrician's office to open one morning. When the doctor arrived and unlocked the door, one young mother remarked, "I suppose to him we look just like a sink full of dirty dishes."

♦ ♦ ♦

The investment counselor was recommending to the 85-year-old man that he purchase a certificate of deposit at 12 percent interest and which matured in 30 months.

"No, thanks," replied the octogenarian. "At my age, I don't even buy green bananas."

♦ ♦ ♦

City officials in Madras, India, are so birth-control conscious that they have an offer for every man who undergoes a vasectomy—$8 plus a week's vacation, eight pounds of rice, and a free movie ticket.

♦ ♦ ♦

An old guy was sitting on a park bench next to a beautiful girl.
"Would you like to have a little fun?" he asked her.
She replied, "How old are you?"
"Eighty-one years old," he says.
She replied, "You've already had your fun."
He says, "I have? How much do I owe you?"

217

The golden moments in the stream of life rush past us and we see nothing but sand; the angels come to visit us, and we only know them when they are gone. —George Eliot

♦ ♦ ♦

Because a fellow has failed once or twice, or a dozen times, you don't want to set him down as a failure till he's dead or loses his courage—and that's the same thing. —George Horace Lorimer

♦ ♦ ♦

"How can I ever show my appreciation?" gushed a woman to Clarence Darrow, after he had solved her legal troubles.

"My dear," replied Darrow, "ever since the Phoenicians invented money there's been only one answer to that question."

♦ ♦ ♦

Husband: "You're always wishing for something you haven't got."

Wife: "What else is there to wish for?"

♦ ♦ ♦

CHINESE FOLK POEM
(c. 2500 B.C.)

When the sun rises, I go to work;
When the sun goes down, I take my rest;
I dig the well from which I drink;
I farm the soil that yields my food.
I share creation; kings do no more.

♦ ♦ ♦

Someone once asked Professor Charles Townsend Copeland of Harvard why he lived on the top floor of Hollis Hall in his small, dusty old rooms. "I shall always live here," he answered. "It is the only place in Cambridge where God alone is above me." Then, after a pause, "He's busy, but He's quiet."

The saddest words on Christmas Eve: "Batteries not included."

♦ ♦ ♦

Husband (to friend): "I want you to help me. I promised to meet my wife at one o'clock for luncheon, and I can't remember where. Would you mind ringing her up at our house and asking her where I am likely to be about that time?"

♦ ♦ ♦

The average person blinks 25 times a minute and scientists say each blink takes one-fifth of a second. Thus, if he averaged 40 miles an hour on a ten-hour motoring trip, he would drive over 25 miles with his eyes shut. —Kalends

♦ ♦ ♦

More Gravestone Epitaphs . . .

From Streatham Churchyard, England:
Here lies Elizabeth, my wife for 47 years, and
this is the first damn thing she ever done to oblige me.

On an old maid who died in the early part of the 19th century in Shrewsbury, Shropshire, England:
Here lies the body of Martha Dias,
Who was always uneasy, and not over pious;
She lived to the age of three score and ten.
And gave that to the worms she refused to the men.

The spinster postmistress of a small town in North Carolina has this epitaph on her gravestone:
Returned—Unopened

Epitaph on Ellen Shannon, age 26, in Girard, Pennsylvania:
Who was fatally burned
    March 21, 1870
by the explosion of a lamp
    filled with "R.E. Danforth's
Non-explosive
    Burning Fluid"

219

A ship in the harbor is safe, but that is not what ships are made for. —J.A. Shedd

♦ ♦ ♦

"Mother," asked a little girl out of a sudden silence, "when will I be old enough to wear the kind of shoes that kill you?"

♦ ♦ ♦

The police officer asked the bank teller, who had been robbed for the third time by the same man, if she had noticed anything specific about the criminal.
"Yes," replied the teller. "He seems to be better dressed each time."

♦ ♦ ♦

The most wasted of all days is the day when we have not laughed.

♦ ♦ ♦

 Liberty is the right to do whatever the laws permit.

♦ ♦ ♦

In order to know the value of money a man must be obliged to borrow.

♦ ♦ ♦

Read the best books first, or you may not have a chance to read them at all. —Henry David Thoreau

♦ ♦ ♦

"What omniscience has music! So absolutely impersonal, and yet every sufferer feels his secret sorrow reached."
—Ralph Waldo Emerson

220

Mankind are always happier for having been happy; so that if you make them happy now, you make them happy twenty years hence by the memory of it.   —Sydney Smith

♦ ♦ ♦

Never give a man up until he has failed at something he likes.
                                                              —Lewis E. Lawes

♦ ♦ ♦

The happiest part of a man's life is what he passes lying awake in bed in the morning.   —Samuel Johnson

♦ ♦ ♦

In a physiology class the teacher said, "Johnnie, can you give a familiar example of the human body as it adapts itself to changed conditions?"

"Yes, ma'am," said Johnnie, "my aunt gained 50 pounds in a year, and her skin never cracked."

♦ ♦ ♦

Life is no brief candle to me. It is a sort of splendid torch which I have got hold of for the moment, and I want to make it burn as brightly as possible before handing it on to future generations.
                                              —George Bernard Shaw

♦ ♦ ♦

He who wishes to secure the good of others has already secured his own.   —Confucius

221

Everywhere I have sought rest
And found it nowhere
Save in little nooks
With books.   —Thomas à Kempis

◆ ◆ ◆

I shall be telling this with a sigh
Somewhere ages and ages hence:
Two roads diverged in a wood, and I—
I took the one less traveled by,
And that has made all the difference.   —Robert Frost

◆ ◆ ◆

When a Frenchman has drunk too much he wants to dance, a German to sing, a Spaniard to gamble, an Italian to brag, an Irishman to fight, an American to make a speech.

◆ ◆ ◆

"I'm glad to find you as you are," said the old friend. "Your great wealth hasn't changed you."

"Well," replied the candid millionaire, "it has changed me in one thing. I'm now 'eccentric' where I used to be impolite, and 'delightfully witty' where I used to be rude."

◆ ◆ ◆

Mother (to small daughter who wants the light left on): "But you sleep in the dark at home, darling."

Small Daughter: "Yes, but it's my own dark at home, Mummie."

◆ ◆ ◆

Justice delayed is justice denied.   —Gladstone

222

INDEXES

TOPIC AND WORD INDEX

A

absence—91
accident report—106
achievement—67, 91, 159
acid—191
acquaintances—51, 198
acting—165, 172, 188, 214
action—28
Adam—168
adjournment—215
admire—84
adolescence—121
adults—37
advancement—67
adventure—47
adversity—71, 97, 113, 206
advertising—44, 46, 177
advice—12, 16, 39, 71, 85, 90, 152, 200
affectation—85
after-dinner speech—122
age before beauty—151
aging—17, 26, 28, 37, 48, 54, 63, 74, 79, 106, 120, 122, 128, 143, 175, 185, 196, 198, 215, 217
agreeability—77
airline luggage—122
airline passenger—99
airlines—93, 199
Alamo—3
Alaska—149
alcohol—16
Alexander the Great—189
Amen—88
America—6, 18, 43, 61, 71, 74, 76, 78, 108, 147
Americans—25, 30, 72, 79, 134, 155, 222
amusement—9, 38, 125, 138
ancestors—121, 130, 175, 195
angels—25, 76, 218
anger—7, 43, 65, 170, 171, 206, 208, 211
animals—109, 195
anniversary—156
answers—169
anticipation—82
antiques—178
anxiety—41
apathy—159
Apollo landing—138
apparel—200
applause—147

Apple microcomputer—99
apples—166, 181
applesauce—198
appointment in Samarra—102
appreciation—20, 36, 118, 218
April—14, 52
archives building—140
argument—108, 159, 163, 166, 204
arise!—61
armies—67
army hitch—121
around the world—199
art—65, 97, 104, 152
Articles of Confederation—185
ash—5
asphalt—76
ass—104
astonishment—121
atheism—49, 110, 206, 211
athletes—54, 137, 194
attaboy!—27
attic—47
attitude—70
auctions—45, 56
Australia—67
author—35, 92
automobiles—30, 52, 60, 97, 123, 163, 192, 199
autumn—125, 131, 140, 148, 161
autumn leaves—158
avarice—198
average—60
awakening—61, 221

B

babies—52, 145, 187
backache—76, 86
bacon—198
bad manners—29
bad times—34
badges—115
baldness—164, 187
ballast—4
Balzac, Honoré de—25
banana—96
band leader—129
bandage—204
bank—161, 210
bank accounts—156
bank director—64
Bank of England—210
bank robber—220
bank vice president—42

225

226

227

false—214
falsehood—36
fame—93, 124, 202
family relations—25, 44, 53, 55, 56, 57, 78, 82, 83, 87, 89, 103, 110, 120, 124, 128, 131, 132, 135, 136, 145, 148, 156, 161, 174, 186, 188, 195, 220
Faraday, Michael—43
farmer's son—97
fashion—36, 62, 73, 132, 145
fast—98
fate—48, 53
father—43, 57, 116, 160, 186
faults—141, 170
favor—197
fear—24, 32, 64, 116, 211
feast—75
feather—146
federal debt—156, 196
fiddle—135
Fields, W.C.—74
fight—66, 222
figure—51, 124
filling station—103
fingers—112
fire—87, 133, 147, 158
Fire and Ice—133
fire drill—147
first amendment—44
first grade boy—103
fish—24
fishing—13, 99, 133
fishing nooks—77
fishing party—11
Flanders Fields—89
flattery—8, 74
flashlight—191
flies—33, 191
flowers—6, 29, 30, 61, 129
flying—188
foe—23
fog—69, 170
food—218
fools—26, 32, 38, 109, 112, 123, 124, 129, 165, 197, 200
foot—182
football—146
football fan—160
footprints on the sands of time—9, 16
for the god of things as they are—19
for whom the bell tolls—12
Ford, Henry—99
forehead—72
foreign—109, 173

foreman—216
forever—50
forget—29, 110
forgiveness—111, 180
fortitude—8, 115
fortune—34, 113, 155, 193, 197
fortune teller—146
forty—196
forty-five—215
founding fathers—76
four urns—135
France—40
Franklin, Benjamin—33, 34, 38, 137, 157, 181, 182, 184, 203, 205
Franklin's 13 subjects—181
free—47
freedom—6, 9, 21, 45, 78, 209
freedom of speech—44
Frenchmen—6, 11, 199, 222
French peasant—65
fresh air—113
fresh fish—85
freshmen—92
fretting—41
friends—7, 19, 24, 46, 49, 51, 64, 68, 70, 75, 92, 108, 111, 116, 123, 125, 130, 131, 132, 137, 153, 163, 197, 211
friendship—51, 108, 110, 177, 178, 211, 215
frost—139
frugality—7, 37, 45, 53, 135, 180, 181, 187, 209
fruit—50, 130, 136
frustration—6, 15, 41, 158, 203
fugitives—154
fun—192, 194, 214, 217
funeral—93
Funk, Wilfrid—76
furnace—23
furniture—56
futility—15, 102
future—17, 83, 202

G

Gallop, George—85
Gandhi, Mahatma—63
gamble—222
gardener—112
garlic—187
geese—139
General—141
generation—204, 211
generous—134

230

231

Hitler, Adolph—23
hobbies—150
hobgoblin—119
hold down—56
hole—65
holiday—196
hollow—71
holly—177
home—107, 176, 191
homeowner—136
homesick—144
honesty—35, 45, 61, 77, 113
honor—26, 108, 118
honorable—69
hope—10, 13, 73, 94, 128, 130, 147
horse vehicles—199
horses—70, 108, 141, 169, 195, 199
hospital—21, 101, 122
hospitality—3
hostility—165
hotel—142
hotel manager—152
house—48, 137
House of Lords—152
housemaid—205
housewife—87
how—40, 46
human—74
human adaptability—221
human behavior—48, 61, 64, 69, 85,
    93, 117, 130, 155, 172, 197,
    204, 210, 211
human beings—82
human body—221
human plumbing—70
human race—36
human rights—23, 70
human voice—104
humiliation—117
humility—17, 26, 32, 33, 60, 76,
    113, 118, 120, 159, 172, 179
humor—86, 172, 176
hunger—206, 209
hunk—76
hurry—79
husband and wife—7, 13, 16, 18, 29,
    31, 46, 55, 76, 81, 90, 93, 94,
    99, 107, 110, 123, 128, 135,
    136, 152, 159, 160, 186, 208,
    215, 216, 218, 219
husbandry—7, 135, 211
husbands—37, 55, 172
hush—76
hyacinth—193
hypocrisy—37, 49, 160, 166
hypocrite—77

I

ice—133, 139
ideals—101
ideas—45, 67, 157, 170, 187, 194
identity—132
idleness—14, 38, 124, 211
ignorance—14, 108, 166
ill measure—109
illegalities—187
ills—197
illustrious—212
imagination—175, 212
imitations—188
immigration—74, 108
immortality—33, 84
impolite—222
impossible—159
In Flanders Fields—89
incentive—85, 90, 103, 116, 121,
    124, 217
independence—187
India—217
Indians—67, 77, 125, 131
indulgence—166
industry—40, 58, 151, 167, 179
inferiority—55
inferiority complex—115
infinity—175
inflation—51, 90, 129, 134, 148
in-flight movies—93
influence—168
information—103, 124
ingenuity—190
ingratitude—117, 131, 177
inheritance—25, 79, 121, 204, 211,
    215
initiative—85
injuries—36, 68
injustice—36
in-kind—67
innocence—214
insomnia—65
installment plan—121
institutions—76, 166
insurance—87, 103, 215
integrity—95, 109, 110
intelligence—4, 57
intercom—101
interest—25, 169
interference—168
international boundary—149
intoxicated—11, 67, 112
inventions—155, 198, 201, 205
investments—217
Irish death bed—53, 119

232

Irishman—222
Irving—153
island—12
Italian—222
Italian restaurant—109

J

Jackson, Andrew—83, 196
jam—50
James I—139
Jane—138
Japanese—155
javelin thrower—137
Jefferson, Thomas—38, 212
jests—109
Jesus—63, 180, 181
Jewish legend—145
Jews—26
Johnson, George—27
jokes—97, 111
joy—113
judges—93, 152, 184
judgment—32, 49, 91, 200
jumper cables—215
jurymen—3
just—69
justice—21, 181, 184, 212, 222

K

kangaroo—67
Kansas—98
key chain—156
kicking—109
kids—102, 105
kill—111
kilts—138
kindergarten—161
kindness—7, 13, 65, 64, 109
kingdom—32
kings—17, 33, 218
kissing—55, 70
kitchen-tested—90
knife—25
knitting—150
knock—82
knowledge—25, 29, 60, 92, 101,
        133, 189, 210, 212

L

labor—50, 60, 82, 97, 163, 212
labor pains—52

labor-saving devices—78
laborer—73
lakes—77
lamp—21, 219
lamp of the mind—206
landscape—153
language—22, 54, 61, 67, 76, 78,
        200
Lardner, Ring—45
laser beams—74
last minute—33
Last Supper—180
last will and testament—47, 79, 99
last words—16
laughter—64, 76, 112, 150, 172,
        194, 201, 220
law—5, 77, 78, 82, 114, 128, 155,
        164, 173, 187, 188, 209, 212,
        220
lawyers—94, 107, 128, 130
laziness—30
leaf—146
leaks—27, 191
learning—64, 184, 189
Lee, Robert E.—124
left—88
left handed—137, 138
leisure—9, 54, 86, 121, 124, 166,
        169, 195
lemonade—110, 212
lending—6, 7, 198
L'envoi—19
letters—27, 90, 165
liar—36
liberty—22, 23, 44, 78, 140, 220
library—5
lies—4, 45, 80, 204
life—200
life and living—10, 38, 40, 43, 46,
        47, 48, 50, 57, 60, 64, 70, 74,
        79, 81, 89, 97, 105, 110, 115,
        123, 165, 169, 174, 185, 190,
        194, 197, 200, 202, 204, 209,
        215, 218, 221
lifting—27
light—168
limburger cheese—187
limitations—180
Lincoln, Abraham—43, 90, 133, 193,
        208, 210, 214
line—149, 182
lion—33
liquor—91
listen—29, 57, 87, 113, 134, 217
Liszt, Franz—205
literature—174

234

236

promotion—56
pronunciation—6
property—60, 128
prosperity—23, 33, 71, 97, 197, 211
protection—30
Protestant—13
Proverbs—214
prudence—23, 32, 129, 209
Psalm 23—7
Psalm 100—140
Psalm of Life—9
pseudonym—95
psychiatrist—102
psychoanalyst—215
public—30, 94
public affairs—40
public appearances—54
public office—117
public opinion—85, 196
public trial—124
punishment—15, 49, 111
pure—69
Puritans—125
purity—150
purse—25, 81
pussyfooting—92
pyramids—177

Q

quack—76
Quakers—200
quality—54, 84, 209
quarrel—200
queens—138
questions—103, 146, 169
quick-freezing—164
quiet—20, 26, 146, 218
quiet minds—50

R

race—34
racetrack—129
radio—46
radium—43
railroads—190, 100
rain—48, 91, 112, 215
rainy day—171, 215
rake—5
rat—137
readiness—74
reading—8, 75, 81, 84, 92, 117, 171
rear ends—87

receiving—112
recommendation—208
reconciliation—169
recruit—125, 207
Red Grange—45
reform—175
refusal—168
regularity—108
rejection—8
rejoice—24, 49
relatives—132
relax—49
religion—26, 138, 155, 211
remember—29, 56, 110
rent—47
repartee—34
reputation—45, 118
Requiem—191
resolution—181
resourcefulness—54, 190
rest—14, 218, 222
restaurant—90, 209
results—52
retirement—108, 131, 194
retorts—89, 94, 142, 165, 176, 207
retreat—162
retribution—66
revenge—5, 17, 47
Revere, Paul—3
revolution—36
reward—210
rice—217
rich—15, 69, 98, 129, 155, 167, 174, 196
ride—169
right—29, 43, 57, 88, 115
ring—215
Ritz—201
river—65, 119, 133
roads—165, 209, 222
robber—96
Rock Ridge—55
rocks—23
rogue—155
roller towel—122
Roman empire—110
Roman statutes—138
romance—11, 86, 162, 164
Roosevelt, Theodore—92
rooster—160
rowing—162
Royal Navy—56
rubber stamp Congress—92
rude—222
rules—42, 121, 149, 215
rum—202

237

238

240

wires—104
Wisconsin—11
wisdom—32, 44, 49, 58, 121, 170,
 173, 193, 200, 210
wise men—109, 113, 124, 173
wishes—52, 144, 171, 218
wit—49
witnesses—158
wives—90
Wizard of Oz—158
women—35, 37, 50, 58, 74, 83, 84,
 87, 90, 97, 108, 111, 132,
 147, 164
wood—5, 94, 111, 183, 189, 207,
 209, 222
wood pulp—207
woodcutter—3
woods—111, 154, 195, 209
wool—98, 171
woolsack—152
words—22, 62, 76, 113, 120, 166,
 200, 212
work—7, 32, 43, 50, 56, 60, 66, 99,
 109, 123, 124, 166, 194, 210,
 212, 214, 216, 218
work clothes—98

work shoes—16
worker—216
working people—60
world—48, 56, 114
worry—67, 79, 169
worship—216
wounds—72, 109
wriggles—117
writing—75, 137
wrong—29, 59, 68

Y

Yale—211
yankee—72
yardwork—136
yeast—94
yesterday—22, 38, 92
Yosemite Valley—202
young—31, 63, 98
youth—26, 169, 170, 198

Z

zoo—195

INDEX OF AUTHORS AND CONTRIBUTORS

Hardy, Thomas—171
Harper's—40
Harris, Sydney J.—170
Harte, Bret—45
Harvey, Paul—28, 61
Hatten, Roy—160
Haughton, Rosemary—141
Hawthorne, Nathaniel—79
Hayes, Helen—79
Henley, William Ernest—53
Henry, Patrick—78
Hepburn, Katharine—108, 214
Herbert, George—91
Herbert, Jack—34
Herschel, Sir John—8
Hindu Proverb—30, 211
Hitchcock, Alfred—68
Hoard's Dairyman—170
Holland, Josiah Gilbert—166
Holman, Ross L.—165
Holmes, John Andrew—69
Holmes, Oliver Wendell, Jr.—146,
    154
Holt, Bishop—122
Hope, Bob—18
Horace—33, 45, 85, 131
Howe, Edward Watson—50, 112,
    123, 163, 191
Hubbard, Kin—124
Hugo, Victor—36, 67, 115, 175
Hunt, Leigh—112
Huxley, Aldous—94, 119
Huxley, T.H.—9, 189

I

Indianapolis News—156
Indianapolis Star—77
Ingersoll—206
Irish Proverb—84
Italian Proverb—96

J

Jackson, Andrew—51
James, William—35
Jefferson, Thomas—9, 22, 70, 83,
    134
Johnson, Samuel—4, 22, 41, 51, 73,
    115, 159, 160, 221
Jolly, A.C.—143
Jones, Barbara A.—48
Jones, Franklin P.—51, 60, 77, 124,
    135, 158

Jonson, Ben—116
Jordan, David Starr—202
Justice, Donald—98

K

Kanin, Garson—109
Kaul, Donald—174
Keats, John—55
Keller, Helen—24
Kelley, James—109, 130
Kempis, Thomas à—222
Kennedy, Ethel—91
Kennedy, John F.—80
Kernan, F.G.—55, 152
Kettering, Charles F.—4, 34, 190
Khayyám, Omar—22
Kipling, Rudyard—19, 107
Kiwanis Magazine—172
Kripke, Rabbi Myer S.—26

L

La Bruyère, Jean de—49
Lamb, Charles—82
Landers, Ann—81, 191
Landor, Walter S.—35
Langenfeld, Byron—176
Lardner, Ring—74
La Rochefoucauld, François, Duc
    de—84, 109, 209
Larson, Doug—112
Lavater—204
Lawes, Lewis E.—197, 221
Leonard, George—53
Leone, Giovanni—35
Levenson, Sam—86, 142
Liebman, Joshua L.—144
Lincoln, Abraham—21, 25, 49, 60,
    72, 115, 129, 162, 167, 190,
    201, 203, 204
Lindbergh, Anne—67
Lombardi, Vince—107
Longfellow, Henry Wadsworth—16,
    57, 91, 104, 198
Lorimer, George H.—218
Louis XIV—97, 117
Lowell, James Russell—165, 168,
    193, 201
Lubbock, John—124
Luther, Martin—143
Lyly, John—81
Lyman Letter—154

245

M

McCrea, Lt. Col. John—89
McDonald, Erwin L.—70
McGinnis, Mack—42
MacFie, Roy Campbell—216
MacLeish, Archibald—204
MacLeod, Alexander—168
Maeterlinck—54
Mangan, James—27
Mann, Horace—71
March, D.—214
Marquis, Donald—194
Masefield, John—80
Matthews, Brander—4
Maugham, W. Somerset—23, 102, 106, 169
Maurois, André—17, 196
May, Albert E.—73
Menander—33
Mencius—214
Mencken, H.L.—4, 84
Mendelson, H.G.—86, 118
Menninger, Karl—102
Michelangelo—166
Millay, Edna St. Vincent—57
Milnes, Richard—113
Mizner, Wilson—29
Moffatt, James—11
Montaigne—217
Moody, D.L.—185
More, Sir Thomas—188
Morley, Christopher—70
Muir, John—175

N

Napoleon I—16, 169
Nash, Ogden—91
Navoi, Alisher—68
Newman, John Henry—174
Nietzsche, Friedrich Wilhelm—40, 97
Northcliffe, Lord—32
Norton, C.F.—142

O

O'Farrell, Ralph W.—41
Old Proverbs—81, 129, 200
Olinghouse, Lane—85
Orben, Robert—168
Osgood, F.S.—198
Otis, Rolland R.—161

P

Pagnol, Marcel—113
Paige, Satchel—66
Paine, Thomas—71
Pascal, Blaise—49, 184
Peale, Norman Vincent—170
Pendenys, Arthur—84
Penn, William—4, 9, 86
Pepler, H.D.C.—128
Pepys, Samuel—100, 169
Percy, Thomas—39
Perry, Oliver H.—91
Persian Proverb—163, 184
Peter, Laurence—5
Pfizer, Beryl—35
Phillpotts, Eden—39
Phoenix Flame—189
Piaf, Edith—87
Pires, Armando S.—30
Pitts, Zazu—150
Pitzer, Gloria—185
Plato—26, 49, 109, 132, 134
Pliny—198
Plutarch—51, 82, 130
Po Chui—153
Polish Proverb—151
Pollock, Channing—4
Pope, Alexander—8, 62, 125
Powell, Lewis F.—124
Price, Lucien—206
Prochnow, Herbert—16
Proust, Marcel—144
Proverbs—166
Psalms—7, 140
Publilius Syrus—183, 197

Q

Quarterly Review, 1825—190

R

Red Fox, Chief—67
Rickenbacker, Eddie—176
Riggs, Austin Fox—193
Roberts, Tom—81
Rogers, Will—46
Romney, George—76
Roosevelt, Eleanor—55, 166
Roosevelt, Franklin D.—37
Roosevelt, Theodore—66, 92
Rootes, Lord—19
Rosenwald, Julius—15
Roskens, Ronald W.—166

Woodring, Paul—32
Wordsworth, William—10, 213

Y

INDEX OF FIRST LINES OF POEMS